Walk, don't run

Walk, don't run

A collection of essays on information issues
published to honour Mrs Edith Körner CBE
Chairman of the NHS/DHSS Health Services
Information Steering Group
1980–84

Edited by
Alastair Mason and Victor Morrison

King Edward's Hospital Fund for London

© King Edward's Hospital Fund for London 1985
Typeset by J & L Composition Ltd,
Filey, North Yorkshire
Printed and bound in England by Oxford University Press
Distributed for the King's Fund by Oxford University Press

ISBN 0 19 7246311

King's Fund Publishing Office
126 Albert Street
London NW1 7NF

CONTENTS

THE CONTRIBUTORS

Michael Alderson is the chief medical statistician at the Office for Population Censuses and Surveys. He was an alternate member of the Steering Group.

John Ashley is a senior medical officer at the Office for Population Censuses and Surveys. He served on all the working groups concerned with information about clinical activity.

Christopher Day is a researcher at the Health Services Management Centre, Birmingham. He is the author of *From figures to facts*, commissioned by the Steering Group.

Bob Dearden is the chief executive of the NHS Training. Authority. He was formerly the district administrator in Hereford, one of the four districts which participated in piloting the Steering Group's recommendations.

Michael Goldacre is director of information services at the Oxford RHA. He was a member of the Steering Group and the working groups concerned with maternity information.

Graham Guest is director of management research at the Wessex RHA. He was a member of the Steering Group and the working groups concerned with information about manpower and diagnostic services.

Stuart Haywood is a senior lecturer at the Health Services Management Centre, Birmingham.

Walter Holland is Professor of Community Medicine at St Thomas' Hospital, London. He was a member of the Steering Group and the working group concerned with information about community health services.

Alan Jennings is a consultant anaesthetist at the Northampton General Hospital. He was a member of the Steering Group and the working groups concerned with information about hospital clinical activity.

David Kenny is the regional general manager at North West

Thames RHA. He was chairman of the working group concerned with the protection and confidentiality of patient and staff data.

David King is the district general manager in Exeter Health District. The district was one of the sites used for piloting the Steering Group's recommendations and he was a member of the working group concerned with information about hospital clinical activity.

Rudolf Klein is Professor of Social Policy at Bath University.

Frances Martin is a member of the Körner implementation team in North Western RHA. She was responsible for coordinating the piloting of the maternity recommendations.

Janet Ousby is a research assistant at the Leeds General Infirmary. She was responsible for coordinating the CAER project.

Vic Peel is the district general manager in Bolton Health District.

Trevor Rippington was until 1984 the regional treasurer at South Western RHA.

Ellie Scrivens is a researcher at Bath University. She was a member of the working group concerned with information about community health services.

Lorna Wainwright is an officer of the NHS Training Authority; she was training officer to the Steering Group. A member of all working groups concerned with hospital clinical activity, she coordinated every pilot study except accident and emergency, and maternity.

Chris West is the district general manager in Portsmouth Health District.

David Wilson is a consultant in the accident and emergency department at the Leeds General Infirmary. He was chairman of the CAER Project Steering Group.

John Yates is a researcher at the Health Services Management Centre, Birmingham.

FOREWORD

The story of the NHS/DHSS Health Services Information Steering Group is well worth telling. Appropriately this volume sets out to do so, not through a single narrative, but through a series of essays by people who were closely involved, or who have particular insights. Thus the picture that emerges is multidimensional, rather than unidimensional. Appropriately also the essays are published in honour of Mrs Edith Körner, who chaired the Group from its beginning until 1984, and with whose name its work is inseparably linked.

The task of overhauling the information systems of the NHS was a daunting one. It had never been done before. I recall at the time of the reorganisation studies in the Department of Health in the early 1970s, a clear conclusion that information systems from periphery to centre needed comprehensive review, and probably radical simplification and redesign. But nobody leapt to commission or undertake the task, which seemed likely to prove fearsomely complicated. As so often, people turned away with exhaustion and relief from major changes of organisation structures, and had little appetite to tackle the systems changes that are their logical corollary. For if structures form the bones of organisations, systems resemble their nerves and sinews.

Patrick Jenkin's decision (when Secretary of State) to commission a full-scale review of health services information was therefore surprising only because it was so long overdue. The form of the review was to be a joint enterprise between the DHSS and the NHS. That seemed appropriate to the task in hand, and was in keeping with the Ministerial mood of that time, reflected in *Patients First*. The emphasis was on greater decentralisation of management in the service, more influence by the periphery on the centre. A major study of information systems at all levels from local to national appeared a 'natural' for a new experiment in joint enterprise, going much beyond traditional patterns of NHS representation on Departmental working parties. To an extent it was a challenge by central government to the National Health Service. Here was a problem of great complexity, important in the running of the service: what could the NHS do about it in a joint enterprise, rather than accepting a centrally imposed solution?

The energy and enthusiasm that this approach released are impressive, as many of the essays in this volume demonstrate. As someone who was barely involved, and is in no sense an information or systems 'buff', I was constantly struck by the missionary zeal with which the team applied itself to what seemed a fairly dry task. Equally impressive was the response from the service. A very large number of very busy people contributed substantially to the endeavour.

At the centre of all this activity was Mrs Körner herself, and a small secretariat headed by Dr Alastair Mason. They formed a winning combination, with a distinctive style of work and complete loyalty and mutual confidence. What they were undertaking called for project management skills of the highest order: breaking the task down into parts, progressing each part, and weaving the conclusions into a single whole. Clarity of ideas was essential – the idea of a basic district information set, for example. So were energy, attention to detail, and practicality, culminating in bench testing in trial districts. Each link in the chain seems obvious enough in retrospect, but each had to be designed, forged and put in place. Throughout, there had to be an unending and passionate commitment to communication, more by word of mouth than in writing, if the many people involved in the initiative were to understand their role, and the service was to accept the results.

So the design and testing phases are now over, completed with great thoroughness and panache, and the old team has dispersed. Mrs Körner, Dr Mason and the rest of the team have emerged from a near-impossible task with honour. Of course much remains to be done if the resulting information is to be accurate and to be used. The baton has passed to others in the new NHS Management Board and in the field. Perhaps I may make two final comments that are not directly connected with the task of implementing the Steering Group's findings. The first is a plea that the energy released by the device of a genuine partnership between the DHSS and the NHS will be remembered. It points to the advantage of challenging people at all levels in the service to take an active rather than a passive role in problem resolution. It also underlines that NHS people and DHSS people can be far more effective working closely together than at arm's length.

The second comment concerns the need to see the Körner reports as an important stage in the continuing evolution of health services information, not as an end-point. It would show a sad unawareness of Mrs Körner's quickness and breadth of mind to allow NHS information systems to set in concrete, rather than continue to develop. For the moment the group has decided to stay with information that is currently available – a perfectly understandable decision, perhaps an essential one. But it leaves some important, neglected territory unexplored, for example concerning the impact of services on levels of health and handicap in the community.

It was Dr Mason who first approached me to ask whether the King's Fund would publish a series of booklets on information issues for the Steering Group. We have been glad to do so and the venture has been a success (including a commercial success). I am delighted that the King's Fund should now be associated with this tribute to Mrs Körner, her team, and all who worked with them in this impressive venture to transform the quality of health services information and its use.

Robert J Maxwell

1

Mrs Körner and her steering group

David King

W ho could have guessed in 1980 that by 1985 the style of NHS management would change from the long established gentle drift of concensus to the riptide of accountability. It is easy to look back now and say that it was inevitable, but in 1980 the possibility was not widely predicted. In those days the NHS had still to be wooed and won to new ideas: the issuing of 'you will' orders through a review system was unthinkable. Though the complexities of health care management may not have changed, what is expected of those appointed to get some order into events has altered radically. In reviewing and assessing the work of the Steering Group on Health Services Information it is important to remember the managerially laissez-faire period in which it was introduced and had to conduct its business. A period when management information was still an optional extra, a fad to which people had to be converted, not an essential requirement for the work to be done.

In such an atmosphere the politicians could be forgiven for expecting more kicks than ha'pence when they decided on an information review. Their anticipation of success could not have been high. But the fates were smiling, for in appointing Mrs Körner to the chair they found a driver for the project with talents uniquely suited to the task and essential for its success. Spring cleaning a cluttered information attic might have seemed the ideal job for a very clever and practical lady, but the assignment was much more than this and to assess what had to be done we shall have to examine the world before Körner.

The good old days

History records that information systems were inaccurate, slow and uncoordinated; little wonder that they were seldom used. The Steering Group's first report describes a 'vicious circle of under use of information and poor quality of the data collected'. After 30 years of the NHS it might seem reasonable to expect the wrinkles to have been ironed out, the systems de-bugged. Why had indifferent arrangements persisted? Was it because the system always defeated the people; or that the people were more ready to find fault with the system than use it?

Certainly, the systems were beset with structural obstacles to their convenient use, many of which stemmed from confusion about ownership and purpose. They had all been introduced to the NHS by the DHSS without much, if any, discussion, negotiation or coordination. Individual disciplines in the NHS had each been commissioned to run separate systems and these charges were faithfully fulfilled by people who assumed that the data were essential for work at the Department. They seldom, if ever, used the information themselves. It would have seemed presumptuous, somehow improper, to adapt and coordinate different systems for local use, when on the slightest aspect of interpretation reference had to be made to the Department. But even in the DHSS no person or office could be located with clear responsibility for any or all of the data flows. Completing the returns was a religious observance, a periodic turning of the prayer wheels, with no expected purpose or reward – at least, in this life.

Another set of obstacles had to do with the technology employed. At the point of entry, manual systems were (indeed, often still are) in evidence so that the manipulation of data was laborious, evening and weekend consuming, and fraught with error. At regional and national data collection centres there were (and are) computers with the characteristics of costive yaks, apparently voracious maws leading to interminable and slow moving digestive systems which sporadically – and much later – engulf the unwary in copious and incomprehensible outpourings. Collecting and processing methods were out of sympathy with all but the most reflective and long term observer of the health scene.

Despite all these impediments there were 'information buffs' who would get the system to deliver, whether it meant using knitting needles to link holed stationery or, latterly, playing with desk top computers. There were even a few virtuosi who could make music with regional main frames. From the chaos of data, messages could be deciphered, for those brave enough to hear what they had to say: and hereby hangs the next part of the tale.

For many the messages were only acceptable if they emphasised the need for more resources; unpalatable if they suggested ineffective stewardship of existing allocations; and beyond the pale should they reveal a need for improved or changed individual performance. That information can be revealing and embarrassing was well known and since no demands were made upon the NHS for private or public self examination, anyone attempting to do so within the system was regarded either as a misguided innocent or more frequently, a trouble-maker. It simply was not cricket! Information, particularly about the way work is done for patients, can rouse passions difficult to quell. It is hardly surprising that the majority have preferred to denigrate the statistics rather than improve them and face the music. Finally, there are professionals, administrators and members who have faith in instinct and mistrust numbers. Mrs Körner once had occasion to chide a fellow member of a health authority who had set aside the quantified information (presumably because it was unhelpful to his argument): 'Would you rather we examine the entrails of a chicken to inform our decisions?' she is said to have asked.

Had Mrs Körner only to deal with data and their conversion into information the task would have been considerable but now we can see why the circle of under use of information and poor quality of data was vicious, because so much human emotion was enmeshed in the systems and their use – it was a minefield. The only way to improve matters in 1980 was by persuasive argument. That Mrs Körner survived with success and plaudit says a lot for her personal qualities.

Mrs Körner

She established her authority by brute ability, being better informed and working harder than anyone else. Everyone accepts that she knows more about the subject and has read more (in several languages) about it than any two other people. It is rare for a chairperson to be so well briefed independently of the secretariat – nobody could pull the wool over her eyes. Hers is not merely a detailed knowledge of a limited technical subject, for her grasp of health services internationally and the changes they are undergoing provides a general context into which the invaluable auxiliary information fits. Mrs Körner's commitment to the task and her capacity for hard work never flagged even when, in addition to everything else, she was found to be rattling over almost every inch of British Rail's tracks to attend or address meetings. Happily, these formidable qualities are leavened with a keen sense of humour, and when Körner activity was in full flood, it was rare to meet any one engaged in it who did not start the conversation with the latest anecdote or bon mot.

Powerful intellect and incisive humour are not always an endearing combination unless, as in her case, they go with a genuine regard for others, whatever their station and ability. This respect and affection for the NHS and those who work for it were apparent to everyone, and people sensed that here was a reformer with her heart in the right place. In consequence many people contributed unstintingly to the work of the Steering Group – how else could it have done its work in so little time? – and very many more were willing to give the results a fair hearing.

Vision there was and expertise; Mrs Körner could manage and communicate. But was there an Achilles heel? In her years at the South Western Regional Health Authority her well informed and impeccably reasoned views did not always carry the day. In 1980, there was real concern among her friends whether she could deliver – bring the NHS to the water and persuade it to drink. Would the report be another learned treatise to gather dust on the shelves? In 1985, we celebrate her success. She made it!

The Körner approach

The formula for this success lay in a shrewd reading of the market and a comprehensive approach to the project based on the practices of commerce rather than public service.

5

Careful attention was given to good design and effective sales, producing what was wanted at the right time and price. The key to this lay in the involvement of large numbers of people drawn from the NHS whose experience and expertise ensured sensibly designed systems and whose commitment helped persuade their colleagues to give the 'thumbs up' to the reports. It was an exercise in participation on a scale unparalleled in the history of the health service. So many people took part or were consulted that the reports when published contained few surprises, they were epilogues to a great cooperative effort. Amazingly, this reservoir of commitment and goodwill existed: Mrs Körner and her secretariat had the wit to tap it and put it to good effect. For a time the Körner activity gave the NHS a common identity of purpose so that at the conclusion of the four year period Mrs Körner had set for the task, implementation did not seem to depend on ministerial instruction, for by then everyone had come to accept that change was inevitable.

Few people understand the structural relationship between the NHS and the DHSS: sufficient to say that it is complex. When committees, working parties and steering groups are formed it is usual for their members to be recruited so as to represent all interests. Despite attempts to achieve balanced representation, however, there is always a suspicion, whether or not it is justified, that the Department manages to exercise a powerful influence on the conduct of affairs in a variety of ways. Since the work of the Steering Group would affect so many aspects of NHS activity and since there were so many potential areas of conflicting interest, Mrs Körner skilfully arranged an organisational position for the group at the junction of the DHSS and the NHS, which was essential if the NHS was to be convinced that it would have real influence.

Secretariats are crucial for the success of committee work and the Civil Service is full of people trained to run them. There is always a danger that officials temporarily seconded are unclear to whom they owe allegiance, especially as they maintain departmental contacts for much of the time. Here, too, Mrs Körner was keen to ensure that the independence of her secretariat was as complete as it could be. She appointed her staff and it was clear to them, and to the branches of the DHSS from which they were seconded, that they were working for her. The choice made available and her skill in spotting people of ability resulted in a small and exceptionally capable group who, with her, were essential to the successful management of the project in all its aspects. They assisted the Steering Group and numerous working parties; tirelessly negotiated with all interests; travelled to discover what was happening and, more importantly who was doing it; and ensured that the lines of communication were always open and attentive.

Knowledge of the service and the effective people working in it was a particular strength of the Körner project. The work of designing data systems and negotiating the information requirements at all management levels from the so called 'sharp end' to the DHSS was assigned to working groups. Although membership of the working groups had to be agreed with a variety of interests, the important starting point was knowing the people with the experience and ability to make an effective contribution.

Most professional groups have a line of communication from the ground to the giddiest organisational heights. A bright doctor working in a hospital or general practice will be known at national level through the BMA, and similar networks exist for nurses, treasurers and administrators. But there is one essential group in a number of information chains who had long remained in the shadows until Mrs Körner put them into the limelight. Medical records had languished under the wing of health service administration, performing essential work but going largely unnoticed and with limited influence. Any lasting reform of information systems required the commitment of medical records officers and their staffs and a great deal was done to ensure that their voice was heard. It was no accident that the only full time member of the secretariat drawn from the NHS was a medical records officer.

Working methods

The working groups were each given a body of information to review and revise. The novel twist was that there was to be no working behind closed doors; interested parties could have access to minutes at all stages. British public servants take some convincing that work is not best conducted in secret, and there was some danger that working openly would inhibit the working groups' activities. However, they soon became accustomed to explaining, consulting and negotiating and, consequently, remained in touch with what was acceptable and therefore possible.

If acceptability was important, so too was affordability. It was crucial not to introduce information demands which would materially increase the costs of collection. Although no specific resource constraints were imposed the experience and judgement of working group members ensured that costs were kept in bounds. The group members worked together in the formidable task of identifying the data to collect, and negotiated hard with each other to agree the information returns that are really necessary for work at each level of the service from district to DHSS. In essence this meant convincing people at higher levels not to request everything 'just in case' they had need of it.

Their tasks completed, the working groups presented the results to the Steering Group, a written examination followed by a tough viva. Then followed something of an inspiration – bench testing of the surviving recommendations in trial districts. This practical test, so obvious in engine design, was an innovation for health service data systems. Long after working group members had laid down to rest, the secretariat slaved on with the trial districts in a process known as piloting, or seeing whether what had been recommended could be put into practice. Volunteer districts and staff were found, willing to try the new systems in addition to their routine information activities. It was at this stage that work began on harnessing the new generation of computers to the business of recording and analysing the Körner systems. Thus the new information products were designed, developed and applied to modern information technology.

Mrs Körner now had to persuade the NHS to accept the recommendations, and she mounted an unprecedented sales campaign which penetrated every part of the service. Magazine articles, video cassettes, interviews and public appearances at annual professional conferences – all were used to spread the word. High level, and not so high level, management meetings were addressed by the lady and her secretariat. The purpose was not to persuade important people that here was something new, to be understood and then explained to the ranks: rather it was to inform them that so many people in the ranks of the NHS had already done so much that it was the duty of important people to enable the new systems to be introduced. They bowed to the inevitable and Körner is now the accepted and author-ised version, replacing all others.

The jig-saw was finally completed by showing people the practical uses of information. Körner Klubs have been established in different parts of the UK with a membership drawn from professionals who need to put information to use. Practical examples are demonstrated and discussed, encouraging the spread of good practice and ideas.

Coda

Mrs Körner was given a formidable task. She set tight timetables for its completion and these were met; the first new systems will be implemented nationally in 1987. The extent of her accomplishment is to have persuaded nearly a million people to a new way of working which should improve the management of the service. Hers was the first major review of the NHS information systems; she has shown that it can be done, and this will be her lasting contribution, an example to all who follow. In July 1984 Mrs Körner resigned from the Steering Group at a high point of her career, but not the end. Being the person she is, her energies are now applied in 'fresh woods and pastures new'. Sadly, not the NHS.

2

The politics of information

Rudolf Klein and Ellie Scrivens

I n discussing the 'information revolution' it is all too easy to become mesmerised by the technological transformation of society. It is tempting to see change in terms of the development and diffusion of hardware and software and the impact of technology on the nature and distribution of work. Yet this is to risk missing what may well be the main significance of what is actually happening – that the 'information revolution' is in fact transforming ways of thinking about political, organisational and social problems, about the structure of government and about the delivery of services.

In this chapter, therefore, we seek to put the work of Mrs Körner and her colleagues into this wider context. Their achievements can only be fully appreciated if they are seen both as a product of, and a contribution to, a shift in styles of thought about government in its widest sense: a shift which is illustrated by the Körner initiative but the significance of which goes well beyond the National Health Service. Our concern is with the 'politics of information': the way in which changing pressures on the NHS and on government are affecting the demand for, and use of, information and what this implies, in turn, for relationships within the NHS and the structure of decision-making. The Körner initiative can be seen as a landmark in documenting these changes.

The timing of the initiative

Any assessment of the Körner exercise must begin with a puzzle. Almost from the birth of the NHS, it was recognised that the organisation lacked anything remotely resembling an adequate information system. This was a theme which emerged repeatedly from countless working parties and committees. The Guillebaud Committee of 1956[1] called for better information so that managers could assess efficiency and 'standards of performance'; the 1972 reorganisation 'Grey Book'[2] pointed out that 'although much information is available at all levels of the service, many improvements will be needed. Existing information is sometimes unreliable, of doubtful relevance and out of date, and there are gaps in what is available ...'; and the Royal Commission report of 1979[3] returned to the charge: 'the information available to assist decision-makers in the NHS leaves much to be desired. Relevant information may not be available at all, or in the wrong form. Information that is produced is often too late to assist decisions and may be of dubious accuracy.' The consensus of opinion is clear. So why did the NHS have to wait until 1980 for the appointment of the Steering Group on Health Services Information and the design of a management information system geared to the needs of a service spending almost six per cent of the nation's resources and employing nearly a million people?

The most likely explanation to observers in 1985 would appear to be the advent of new technology making it at last possible to analyse and distribute information to more people, more rapidly and more cheaply than ever before. However, the history belies this. Although the Department of Health and Social Security had been grappling with the problems of information technology since the 1960s, albeit with a conspicuous lack of success,[4] cheap and easily accessible information technology only appeared on the NHS scene after the Steering Group had begun its task. The Körner exercise in fact predates the widespread involvement of the NHS in computing, although it post-dates the beginning of the complex policy discussions about computing and information technology.

Any rational model of policy making would suggest that something like the Steering Group should have been launched at least a decade earlier, for two reasons. Firstly the documentary evidence cited above indicates that the need for such work was universally recognised. Secondly, the growing awareness of the uses and accessability of information technology should have meant the design of an appropriate information system preceding, not following, the debates about information technology. The need to think through the conceptual basis and practical design of an information system – the real, daunting task of the

13

Steering Group – was evident long before information technology became a NHS concern.

A different explanation of the timing of the Körner initiative is that it followed a breakthrough in the collective intellectual capacity of both the DHSS and the NHS to make use of information. Against the background of the litany of complaints about inadequate information in the NHS there existed a pervasive scepticism about the usefulness of information. This is well described in Enoch Powell's reflection in 1966 on his time as Minister of Health:

> Enormous effort has been lavished during the twenty years of the National Health Service on the collection of statistics of hospital activity, and on the search among them for the means of making valid comparisons, within the service itself and between the service and other systems. It is a search I myself engaged in with the freshness and hopefulness of inexperience, only to be driven into recognising reluctantly that the search was inherently futile. The most carefully constructed parallels between one hospital or hospital group and another dissolved on closer examination into a baffling complex of dissimilarities. Every attempt to apply a common standard had the effect of disclosing a deeper level of individual differences and incommensurables.[5]

In subsequent years there have been attempts to devise new and more sophisticated instruments of measurement – particularly by economists[6] – but these have never moved beyond the development stages. Whatever prompted the creation of the Steering Group, therefore, had as little to do with new techniques for deriving information as it did with the availability of new technology.

The real explanation for the Körner initiative is, as we shall suggest in the remainder of this chapter, more complex. The crucially relevant factor was not change in information technology nor information production, though these obviously played some part, but change in the political and economic environment in which the NHS operates.

The task allocated to the Steering Group is significant because it reflected a change in the perception of the issues involved in the running of the NHS. Correspondingly, the long term significance of the Körner contribution to the NHS will have to be evaluated in terms of how the information systems are used and by whom.

Information of itself has little value. It is a tool to be used to aid decision-making and to monitor and perhaps improve performance of tasks. It proves the basis for accountability in an organisation and, as such, is enmeshed in its functioning and management. Therefore, the Körner exercise cannot be viewed simply as neutral and technocratic but as something which raises fundamental questions about accountability within the NHS organisation. Who is accountable to whom; what should the currency of accountability be; and how should power within Britain's health care system be distributed, both between the different levels in the administrative hierarchy and between the different professional groups responsible for running the service? It is this dimension of the Körner exercise which makes it of interest to all those involved in the process of government in the eighties.

Efficiency and accountability

In the sixties, and to a lesser degree in the seventies, expenditure planning for the NHS – as indeed for all public services – was based on expectations of economic growth. In the eighties, these plans were revised to take account of the reality of economic stagnation, a trend further reinforced by the Conservative government's bias against increasing public expenditure and, correspondingly, for cutting taxation. The result was a drive for greater efficiency and a search for greater accountability, the pressure coming part from central government, part from Parliament. But as it turned out information was what both needed in order to achieve their aims, if for somewhat different reasons.

If money is short, one obvious response is to make what

is available go further by increasing the efficiency with which it is used. Predictably, one response of the Government to economic stringency has been to invoke the language of 'value for money'. This has been directed at all government departments, including the NHS, as the 1983 White Paper on Financial management in government departments indicates:

> Total public expenditure in 1983–84 is expected to be 43% of the gross domestic product. It is the Government's aim to contain this growth in order to curb taxation and borrowing. It is thus essential that resources should be used efficiently and public money spent wisely. ... A sense of responsibility for achieving value for money must be widely disseminated in the government service.[7]

Dissemination of the sense of responsibility was to be achieved through ensuring that managers at all levels should have 'a clear view of their objectives'; and means to assess, and wherever possible measure, outputs or performance in relation to these objectives. And, of course, this involved 'the systematic assembling of basic information about the objectives of existing policies' and 'criteria or targets against which to assess results and the costs'.

For the NHS, the policy took the form of imputing 'efficiency savings' when calculating the allocation of funds. That is, the Government assumed that any expansion of the service required in response to demographic or other pressures would be financed, in part at least, by internally generated savings. 'Value for money' became the vogue in the NHS, as in the rest of the public sector.

The logic of financial stringency was not only to reinforce the drive towards increased managerial accountability within the public sector, the message of the 1983 White Paper, but was also to create demands for greater political accountability – the message of a succession of parliamentary reports.[8] If Ministers were making their plans for the NHS on the assumption that increasing efficiency was financing the continuing expansion of the service, then MPs wanted to be provided with the evidence to show that this was indeed the case, and that the efficiency savings were not merely a euphemism for cuts in the quality or adequacy of services. From the Public Accounts Committee and the Social Services Committee of the House of Commons there came an insistent barrage of criticism of the DHSS, in particular of the Department's seeming inability to find out (let alone control) what was happening in the NHS as a result of its expenditure and other policies.

Nowhere are the counterbalancing forces of decentralisation and central accountability more apparent than in the report of the NHS management inquiry team led by Mr Roy Griffiths. The recommendations suggest that the 'accountability review process should be extended right through to unit management', and, at the same time 'that all day-to-day decisions be taken in the main hospitals and other units of management'.[9]

The logic of both managerial and political accountability point in the same direction; more and better information. The 1980 report of the Social Services Committee concluded emphatically that 'the DHSS should give high priority to developing a comprehensive information system which would permit this committee and the public to assess the effects of changes in expenditure levels or patterns on the quality and scope of services provided'.[10] Moreover, it stressed that 'the ability of Parliament to make a reality of ministerial accountability depends on the availability of appropriate information'. Equally significant were the responses by the Government, and by the Public Accounts Committee.[11] Wearing 'sack cloth and ashes', the DHSS replied:

On coming into office Ministers were quickly aware that the data base on which HPSS (Health and Personal Social Services) monitoring rests was unsatisfactory. It appeared that much of the information collected was now of little value, while information of potentially greater value including more useful costing information, was lacking. Accordingly, they launched a number of studies. First, a NHS/DHSS group chaired by Mrs Körner, Vice-Chairman of the South Western RHA, was appointed to look at health services information. . . .

Thus we return to the genesis of the Steering Group on Health Services Information: a combination of pressures generated partly by government and partly by Parliament, within an economic and political environment in which it could no longer be taken for granted that the continuing expansion of NHS services would be financed by the dividends from national economic growth. The 'inherently futile' search for better information, to use Enoch Powell's phrase, had suddenly become of vital importance.

Centralisation or decentralisation

The economic imperative offers the most plausible explanation for the timing of the creation of the Steering Group, but the rationalisation of information systems also reflects and contributes to one of the enduring tensions within the management of the NHS: the tension between central control and local responsibility. If the Secretary of State for Health and Social Services is accountable to Parliament for the running of the NHS, does it not follow that he has to be assured that health authorities are spending public money in a manner which is acceptable not only to himself and his government but to Parliament?

The solution would appear to be close central control of health authority activity, although this conflicts markedly with the philosophy of devolved responsibility for actions and decision-making which has characterised Conservative government policy towards the NHS.

> We are determined to see that as many decisions as possible are taken at the local level – in the hospital and in the community. We are determined to have more local health authorities whose members will be encouraged to manage the service, with the minimum of interference by any central authority, whether at region or in central government departments. We ask that our proposals be judged by whether they achieve these aims. . . .[12]

These proposals formed the basis for the 1982 reorganisation of the NHS. There may be a certain irony in recalling the rhetoric which accompanied this reorganisation, given the subsequent preceptorial role adopted by the DHSS and the authoritarian tones in which instructions have been issued to health authorities on such issues as contracting out. However, there remains the question of whether the Steering Group's proposals are to be implemented as part of the original intention to devolve responsibility or whether the implementation is to be seen as a reversion to a centralist mode of organisation.

Which will be the reality is yet to be seen. On the one hand, better information improves the ability of central government to know what is happening at the periphery, and thus to call health authorities to account for what they are doing. On the other hand, better information can transform the nature of the relationship between the centre and the periphery, allowing the periphery responsibility for the type and content of its decisions whilst keeping the centre, routinely and therefore unobtrusively, informed of its actions. A better information system may permit the DHSS to exercise control without the kind of detailed, day to day intervention in the affairs of health authorities which in the past has generated so much resentment.[13] This is the view taken by the Social Services Committee which argued that the easier it is to compare the overall performance of individual health authorities, the less need there is to scrutinise their decisions in detail.[14] A better information system is one way of reconciling the conflicting needs of NHS accountability to Parliament and decentralisation of decision-making.

In short, the purpose to which information is put in the NHS is the issue at stake. The same information system can be used to support the philosophies of centralisation or decentralisation with equally convincing arguments. This is because, as discussed earlier, information is simply a tool for management, and its influence is tied, not to the information per se, but to its interpretation. Within the NHS, the interpretation of data is never obvious. Not only can information convey different meanings to different professional or occupational groups but, in addition, as Enoch

Powell found, the opportunities for claiming that no two consultants, hospitals or health authorities are comparable, are endless.

Ways of insisting that data are comparable are being sought. Improvements in the quality of the data, their frequency of production and content are under discussion. Considerable effort is being put into refining items of data so that claims of uniqueness are invalidated. However, at the end of the day success will be dependent upon denying the reality of the claims, and changing attitudes towards interpretation, rather than altering the information itself.

Inevitably, therefore, the work of the Steering Group is only a part of a dialogue about the way in which the NHS is managed. Other initiatives in the information field have also begun, which reflect this trend. There is, for example, the DHSS performance indicator exercise, institutionalised in the performance review system. The DHSS uses information to 'challenge health authorities' – in the words of Sir Kenneth Stowe, Permanent Secretary to the DHSS, to the Public Accounts Committee.[15] The information gives the DHSS greater leverage, in the sense of enabling it to ask more searching questions. What is valid information does not have to be defined at this juncture since the exercise is seen simply as promoting discussion. In addition, the interpretation of ambiguous information is also left open in the continuing dialogue between the central organisation and the peripheral district health authorities.

The politics of the post-Körner era

The work of the Steering Group was to identify a minimum data set to be used routinely for management purposes in every health authority and in the DHSS. Why the work was considered necessary can be seen as a response to a variety of political and economic influences. How the outcome of the work – the recommendations – will be implemented, and the uses to which the information will be put, will undoubtedly also be the product of political and economic influences. Not only can raw data be open to a variety of different interpretations, they can be combined and 'massaged' to produce a whole range of secondary data, or indicators, which are even more difficult to interpret than the original numbers. The techniques for creating complex indicators are growing daily. Their meaning, and how they will be used, is not clear, though undoubtedly they will begin to enter the armoury used to fight management battles.

The Griffiths report calls for a 'fully developed management budget approach . . . to prompt some measurement of output in terms of patient care'. Not only is the information to be used to promote the measurement of output – a very difficult and sensitive issue in the field of health care – but to 'ensure that the time at present spent by doctors in meetings, committees, etc., will be reduced and employed more purposefully'.[9] At the same time Griffiths calls for clinicians to participate fully in decisions about priorities in the use of resources. It is not clear whether information in this context is a means to control clinicians' behaviour, or a form of morse code to tell them what is going on without their having to attend meetings.

We do not know if information will become a tool to help local decision making; a carrot to induce better district performance by comparisons between districts; or a stick to beat health districts who perform differently from others. It is clear that the real battle over the value and the purpose of information in the NHS has not been finished by the work of Mrs Körner and her colleagues; it has only just begun.

REFERENCES

1 Committee of enquiry into the cost of the National Health Service. Report. (Chairman C W Guillebaud.) Cmnd 9663. London, HMSO, 1956.

2 Department of Health and Social Security. Management arrangements for the reorganised National Health Service. London, HMSO, 1972.

3 Royal Commission on the National Health Service. Report. (Chairman, Sir Alec Merrison.) Cmnd 7615. London, HMSO, 1979.

4 Scrivens E. The impact of information technology: past, present and future trends. Report. Presented to the King Edward's Hospital Fund for London, 1984.

5 Powell J Enoch. Medicine and Politics. London, Pitman Medical, 1976.

6 Williams A. Measuring the effectiveness of health care systems. British Journal of Preventive and Social Medicine, 1974, vol 28, no 3. 196–202.

7 Treasury. Financial management in government departments. Cmnd 9058. London, HMSO, 1983.

8 Day P and Klein R. The ambiguity of accountability. London, Tavistock. (Forthcoming.)

9 Department of Health and Social Security. NHS management inquiry. (Leader, Mr Roy Griffiths.) London, DHSS, 1983.

10 House of Commons Social Services Committee. The Government's White Papers on public expenditure: The social services. Third Report, session 1979–80. HC 702. London, HMSO, 1980.

11 Department of Health and Social Security. Reply by the Government to the Third Report from the Social Services Committee, session 1979–80. Cmnd 8086. London, HMSO, 1980.

12 Department of Health and Social Security and Welsh Office. Patients First. London, HMSO, 1979.

13 Department of Health and Social Security. Regional chairmen's enquiry into the working of the DHSS in relation to regional health authorities. Report. London, DHSS, 1976.

14 House of Commons Social Services Committee. Public expenditure on the social services. Third Report, session 1980–81. HC 324. London, HMSO, 1981.

15 House of Commons Committee of Public Accounts. Financial control and accountability in the National Health Service. Seventeenth Report, session 1981–82. HC 375. London, HMSO, 1982.

3

General management: the information requirement

Chris West

The observation that some problems are important whilst others are urgent is frequently used to illustrate the dilemma of managerial priorities. Like many succinct statements it is an over-simplification, but it contains an important message for NHS managers.

At a time when the NHS is being fundamentally affected by the establishment of the general management function, it may be unrealistic to expect the development of information services to rank high on a general manager's task list. Yet the demands facing managers in the service are of such a scale and penetration that the general manager who fails to treat this subject as an urgent and important priority may well find that his belated attention to information services will, unhappily, coincide with the completion of his fixed term contract.

Accountability

The implementation of the proposals in the Griffiths report[1] has introduced a new management climate in the NHS. The recently introduced annual review system requires health authorities to be accountable for the operation of services within their district or region to a degree not encountered before. The degree of accountability will inevitably tighten as the Government requires the service to demonstrate in explicit terms the net added benefit to patient care of any additional investment that the NHS gains from the Treasury. New measures of performance will soon become common, such as unit cost per case on a standardised case mix; number of in-patient days per £100,000 capital invested; levels of improved productivity in terms of unit labour costs; and the marginal cost per case on a standardised case mix against comparable NHS and private facilities in the locality.

Ministers have made clear the objectives of the annual review process and the accountability reviews. Whilst the accountability reviews have been qualified by a statement that 'they are not intended to oversee every facet of activity', they are nevertheless a process by which health authorities will establish targets, measure performance and review progress. The impact of the reviews and the introduction of a more assertive management process will require tight and responsive management control in the district. This can only be done by having adequate and reliable information.

Technology and skills

Society today has changed dramatically with the impact of micro-processors and the ubiquitous chip and it is important to reflect on the changes that have occurred within the NHS during the last ten years in order to try to predict where they are leading.

At the end of the 1970s, the South West Thames Regional Health Authority and the Oxford Regional Health Authority established their own independent regional computer units with main frame processing facilities, completing a national programme based on standardised configurations of the ICL 1900 series machines. Although this major element of the DHSS standardisation policy was successfully introduced, the policy itself has never been fully implemented.

It is now possible to buy for less than £20,000 a desk top machine with the processing capacity of Oxford's main frame machine which more than seven years ago cost over £500,000. It also required more than 70 support staff, operated in a very tightly controlled air conditioned environment and was housed in a building that cost over one million pounds to erect.

For many purposes the software required for the machine in the £20,000 range does not need the services of the groups of systems analysts and programmers that were essential for the main frame machine. Much of the software can be bought tailor-made, or is already available within the NHS. By 1994 it is likely that no regional health authority will be providing computing services to district health authorities. This is not to suggest the one main frame unit per region will be replaced by 10, 15 or 20 depending on the number of districts in each region. Instead, the processing of information will be undertaken in three different ways. Business systems, such as payroll, may well be undertaken by banks and other information processors that enjoy the benefits of massive economies of scale. Districts will use small computers linked in a series of networks to undertake a range of jobs, many of them operational tasks like the maintenance of waiting lists, the production of booking and admission lists and the creation of accident and emergency department record cards. These operational systems will provide the raw data for the control systems used by managers. Finally there will be machines solely concerned with the provision of analytical support for diagnostic and other equipment.

To benefit from the shift in hardware patterns district managers must consider the range of manpower skills required to capitalise on developments. The NHS must not embark on an ambitious programme to recruit more programmers and analysts. Given its low pay rates, the NHS cannot compete effectively in the labour market for computer staff and it is unlikely ever to do so, even after the fundamental reforms of performance related pay systems and local pay bargaining. The strategy must be to acquire software and software support from the commercial sector.

Although collaboration with the private sector will be challenging, two other changes will have more far reaching consequences. The first will be to train clerical and supervisory staff to dispense with paper based systems and learn to use computer keyboards and visual display units. Secondly, there will be a pressing need to train managers to use quantitative information routinely in their jobs. The implications of both changes should not be underestimated. Modifications in industrial relations law and industrial relations practice exposed appalling weaknesses in NHS management in the 1960s, and rapid developments in information technology could do the same in the 1990s.

General management

NHS managers will no longer be able to afford to wait passively for the production of either a nationally developed information system or a regional computer centre's latest offering. It will be for managers at district level to define their needs and to identify the information required to discharge the responsibilities for which they are accountable. They will need to define precisely much of the information currently enjoying seclusion under the heading 'soft' or 'intuitive'. General managers at all levels will have to face up to these questions.

a) How do you discharge your responsibilities?
b) What information do you use on a routine basis to judge the performance of your unit/district/region?
c) What are your key objectives?
d) What are the critical success factors?
e) What information is used to judge performance against the critical success factors?

Given that the general management function is only now being recognised in the NHS, it may seem unfair to expect managers in such a complex non-trading organisation to produce answers to these questions. But our current expenditure of £16.5 billion a year requires justification. Taxpayer's money must be used effectively and efficiently. Above all, the aims and objectives must be clear at district level. The abolition of district management teams and the appointment of district general managers and unit general managers will provide a clear line of accountability. Chief officers who exercised a degree of assumed authority over unit staff through membership of the DMT will not do so in the future. Post-Griffiths, they will provide information and advice to the district general manager, and assume a supporting role to unit general managers, who will be left to make their own decisions.

Besides defining responsibilities, objectives, critical success factors and information requirements, district managers will have to strike a suitable balance between making better use of information for management purposes and pursuing a degree of perfection that requires painstaking and time-consuming research on every issue. Managers will have to learn to use imperfect information wisely.

The precise organisational arrangements to bring this about cannot be prescribed in a way to suit every authority, but certain general characteristics are clear. The development of information services requires the overt commitment and involvement of general managers. Essential to this commitment is the appointment of a senior manager, having immediate and direct access to the district general manager, with the overall responsibility for managing information services. This appointment may seem a luxury, but the following points are worth noting. First, it is only by the appointment of a senior manager at second-in-line level that authority will be available to ensure that the organisational changes required are achieved. Secondly, given that up to 60 per cent of the total resources of most organisations is consumed by the activities of data collection, storage, analysis, manipulation and communication, it is sensible to appoint a senior person to carry out the necessary changes in information production. Thirdly, the role of the senior information manager will encompass all types of information, be it clinical, financial, manpower, or about capital assets and equipment.

The King's Fund publication *Developing a district IT policy*[2] suggests that this senior manager should be regarded as operating like a 'general practitioner' in information services, able to prepare an operational requirement and systems specification, and to relate to a wide range of users in the role of guide and counsellor. A practical knowledge of information technology and the range of specialist advice available are also desirable; as would be the ability to undertake a limited amount of programming.

Conclusion

For several years it has been recognised that the traditional way of constructing information systems and collecting data in the NHS needs to be changed. The emphasis has to shift from systems based on functional activities to a total system concept based on patients and other target populations. This approach will provide the basis for effective management control and planning.

The task of completely reforming a health authority's

information system is daunting, but it is a job now facing every authority in the country. However, it is only the beginning! The next step will be to learn how to use the information assertively but constructively.

The improved managerial performance heralded by the Griffiths Report[1] depends on the work done by the Steering Group. It has achieved results that, at the outset, I thought was beyond the reach of the NHS and its managers. Setting up a structure in which managers are given responsibility and held accountable, and provided with information to enable them to carry out their duties, should eventually produce a better managed, lower cost, more sensitive and appropriate service. The beneficiaries will thus be the communities and patients the NHS exists to serve.

REFERENCES

1 Department of Health and Social Security. NHS management inquiry. (Leader, Mr Roy Griffiths.) London, DHSS, 1983.
2 Department of Health and Social Security. Steering Group on Health Services Information. Developing a district IT policy. London, King's Fund, 1983.

IMPROVING THE DATA
ENVIRONMENT

4

The training and educational consequences of the work of the Steering Group

Lorna Wainwright
and Bob Dearden

The Steering Group and the NHS Training Authority have faced two common issues. Both bodies were set up as part of the devolution exercise put in train by Patrick Jenkin when he was Secretary of State. The transfer of functions from the Civil Service to other bodies reporting directly to Ministers is fraught with transitional problems. Both bodies were also dealing with aspects of health service management about which there had been much talk and discussion but less action. Considerable lip service has been given to the need for a trained workforce and for information to improve managerial performance. The devolution of the responsibility for training and information provided new opportunities to achieve these aspirations.

The Steering Group

From the start, the group recognised that if managers were to improve their use of information the statistics they used had to be credible. A key factor in producing believable information is trained staff aware not only of how to do it but also why they are doing it. Training and education were seen as crucial elements in the production of an environment in the NHS sympathetic to the proper collection, collation and processing of statistical data and the production and transmission of information derived from them.

Although the major training task was to ensure the smooth implementation of the new national data sets, it was recognised that initiatives should not cease once the new systems had been instituted. The information required by a health authority changes as clinical and management practice changes. Staff enter and leave the organisation. To ensure that information remained credible, authorities would have to set up permanent arrangements to ensure that the staff involved were equipped to do their jobs effectively.

The Steering Group launched two major initiatives. One aimed at training the staff involved in collecting data; the other at staff concerned with the specialist tasks of producing information and implementing systems using information technology.

In each district a large number of staff from many disciplines are involved in the initial recording of data. All managers are, or will be, involved in collecting data about their staff. Data about clinical activities are recorded by a variety of staff including health professionals as well as administrative personnel working in hospital and outside. A prime concern of the group was to improve the quality of clinical activity information. Not only is it concerned with our product – patient care – but also data about clinical activity are an essential component of financial information systems. An important consequence of the group's work has been the general recognition that financial information is only as good as the clinical activity data from which it is derived.

Collecting clinical activity data

The major clinical services provided by a district health authority are shown in Table 1 on page 34. The personnel responsible for collecting data about them differ from one district to another. Data about activity in the wards may be recorded by nurses, clinical support staff or clerks, although the data will always be collated by medical records staff. Operating theatre activity, on the other hand, is usually recorded by nurses in a register and few districts have regular arrangements for collating the data recorded. Services, such as dietetics and occupational therapy, rarely have clerical staff and the recording and collating of data have to be done by the health professionals themselves.

Formal training activities for staff involved in collecting data cannot be instituted until there is an explicit organisational framework for maintaining the quality of the data collected. The Steering Group has proposed[1] that each authority should set district-wide standards for data accuracy, completeness and timeliness, and that managers should be responsible for the quality of data produced by their staff. An important component of these responsibilities is that managers of clinical areas, such as an operating theatres manager or a chief physiotherapist managing a clinical service, are responsible for ensuring that their staff

Table 1: Major areas of clinical work

a. *Services provided on hospital premises:*
   hospital wards
   operating theatres
   accident and emergency departments
   radiotherapy departments
   diagnostic services

b. *Services provided on or off hospital premises:*
   consultant out-patient clinics
   day care facilities
   paramedical services
   maternity services
   family planning services

c. *Services provided in or for the community:*
   preventive services
   community nursing
   child health and school health services

are trained to collect data. These managers will not necessarily carry out the training themselves; in most cases it will be performed by district training staff and staff expert in the production of data.

Having clearly identified the responsibility for training, the group turned its attention to how a central body might best help managers in a district to fulfil their responsibilities. Two complementary training needs were identified. First, staff need to know why information is important; why accurate and complete data collection is essential; and why major changes are being made as a consequence of the implementation of the Steering Group's reports. To help managers motivate their staff, two national training packs have been produced. Each pack contains notes on talking to an audience, a video to introduce the training session, briefing notes and transparencies to be used to structure discussion. The first package, 'What's going on?', describes the need for change and the work carried out by the

Steering Group. The second, 'Can you believe it?', high-lights the importance of collecting credible information.

The second training need is to make staff technically competent. A *User's Guide*, written for use at all levels of the service, contains the minimum data sets and their de-finitions and classifications simply set out in non-technical language. In parallel with the production of the *User's Guide* a set of computer assisted learning (CAL) programs has been developed. These programs, designed to run on the BBC micro B computer, utilise its graphics capability and contain questions to test the learner's acquisition of knowledge. An important by-product of CAL is that staff become accustomed to a computer keyboard and visual display unit.

Educating information specialists

The group has identified two particular skills required in each district to facilitate the production of information: the ability to convert data into information[2] and to implement information technology.[3] For some years, a number of dis-tricts have had information officers concerned mainly with analysing data about hospital clinical activity. Their skills should now be extended to deal with the analysis of all the data recommended in the Steering Group's reports, as well as with the design of surveys and the presentation of in-formation in a professional manner.

Besides their technical competence, effective district in-formation officers require considerable behavioural skills to enable them to find out from senior managers the informa-tion they want, and to satisfy them.

As districts take control of their own information tech-nology (IT) it becomes essential that on-site advice and support is available. Some districts have appointed a dis-trict IT officer with a general knowledge of the capabilities of information technology and the personal and organi-sational skills to collaborate with users when introducing IT applications.

The educational needs of these information specialists

has been met by the Steering Group promoting two courses. Warwick University has a day release course leading to a university diploma which is now in its second year, and in London the King's Fund College took on its first students in January 1984.

The NHS Training Authority

Since September 1984, staff training has become the responsibility of the NHS Training Authority who will maintain the programmes and products initiated by the Steering Group. Two advisory bodies have been set up to continue the work started by the Steering Group. The method of training data collectors has been confirmed and work has now begun on the production of a *User's Guide* and computer assisted learning programs for the manpower and community activity data sets. The need to maintain the confidentiality of patient and staff data was highlighted by the passing of the Data Protection Act in 1984, and a training package to make staff more aware of confidentiality is in preparation.

The education of information specialists requires a comprehensive review. Traditional groupings by discipline, such as specialists in community medicine (information), regional statisticians and information officers are no longer appropriate now that information is being managed as a corporate resource. Before further educational initiatives are launched it will be necessary to establish what sorts of organisational arrangements are required in districts and regions for information handling, the tasks that need to be done and the skills that will be required. The Steering Group made a start by sketching out the progress of current developments. When the district restructurings caused by the Griffiths proposals have been completed it will be easier to identify the long-term educational requirements of the new information specialists.

The Steering Group recognised the importance of educating managers to use information. Indeed in the first report to the Secretary of State it is emphasised that 'the key criterion by which our performance must be assessed is the extent to which information derived from the data sets is used to make decisions about the allocation, planning and review of resources'.[4] Educating managers in the use of information has become the responsibility of the NHS Training Authority. An advisory group has been set up, drawing on the experience of senior staff involved with the Steering Group, the implementation of the Griffiths report and the Performance Indicators Group, to seek the best ways of helping senior managers use quantitative management techniques. The outcome this year will include core curriculum material for management development programmes, speakers' packs and a major investment in an open learning system developed with Henley Management College. The learning system will provide a modular route through the precepts and practices of management information and information technology and will use health service management issues as case studies.

Conclusion

The work of the Steering Group has put information firmly at the top of the management agenda. Its emphasis on training and education and the initiatives it has launched, particularly those using modern educational technology, have given the NHS Training Authority a flying start. If the latter's work proves as useful and acceptable as has that of the Steering Group, we will be well pleased.

REFERENCES

1 Department of Health and Social Security. Steering Group on Health Services Information. Making data credible. London, King's Fund, 1984.
2 Department of Health and Social Security. Steering Group on Health Services Information. Converting data into information. London, King's Fund, 1982.
3 Department of Health and Social Security. Steering Group on Health Services Information. Developing a district IT policy. London, King's Fund, 1983.
4 Department of Health and Social Security. Steering Group on Health Services Information. First Report. A report on the collection and use of information about hospital clinical activity in the National Health Service. (Chairman, Mrs Edith Körner.) London, HMSO, 1982.

5

Information technology

Vic Peel

This essay is a brief description of the Steering Group's contribution to the development of information technology (IT); it is not an analysis. I was fortunate to be party to some of the events of the last six years and comment as a member of the chorus rather than from centre stage. Because I did not appear in every act, my view is incomplete.

The group faced three particular problems. There was an unnecessarily complex relationship between the group and others responsible for IT policy; the uncertainty about implementation which existed until 1984 hindered the development of cost-effective coordinated computer systems; and managers were slow to accept the need for a national minimum data set for management purposes, and for investment in the supporting technology.

The implementation of the recommendations of the Griffiths report[1] should create a management culture which will expedite the introduction of IT founded on Körner-based information. However, progress will be frustrated if there is no resolution of the confusion, with us for many years, caused by the diffuse, ill-defined and often overlapping responsibilities for the nationwide development of the necessary personnel and technological support.

Historical background

The response to the DHSS consultative document about NHS information arrangements,[2] issued in 1979, was the first occasion on which districts had the opportunity to comment on these important issues. They pointed out that the regional computer systems were used for the most part to meet the requirements of the parliamentary process, not the needs of the NHS or the management purposes of the DHSS. It was ironic that, despite the pre-eminence of the Department's requirements, the mass of data available to ministers were out-of-date, inaccurate and incomplete; it often proved impossible to deal adequately with parliamentary questions and with requests for information about the relative performance of authorities.

The data demanded by the DHSS about activity, manpower and finance were the product of a variety of professional disciplines with different concepts and needs. There was an unnecessary separation at all levels between the people running the different data systems and between those responsible for collecting and processing data.

These comments from the NHS were an important factor in the creation of the Steering Group in 1980 with the explicit remit to review not only the data but to provide 'the accepted route for seeking changes to, or developments in, health information systems'.[2] However, the wide terms of reference failed to distinguish between the respective responsibilities of the group and the DHSS which maintained control over NHS computing policy. Once the group started to encourage local information rather than national standard systems, it was inevitable that confusion would lead to frustration.

In the late 1970s, the DHSS was having considerable problems with managing developments in computing and other information technology. Health service computing policy had been established in 1971. ICL mainframe computers were installed in one computing centre in each region and the priority applications were payroll, hospital activity analysis and the provision of statutory accounts. By the end of the decade this limited centralist approach was failing to meet the increasing information needs of districts and areas. Neither the DHSS nor regions were thinking about funding or providing skilled manpower for area or district computing applications.

Matters were brought to a head in 1980 by the resignation of several members of the DHSS Computing Committee, the body with formal responsibility for research and development, because of the DHSS refusal to fund the development of PROMIS in a London teaching hospital. PROMIS, a system developed in America, provides a data capture and processing facility for clinical use through real-time interactive terminals accessed by users in wards and departments. This application for funds and its rejection is of interest for three reasons. Firstly, the bid was for DHSS research monies – computing developments were still being evaluated in a research context rather than a managerial one. Secondly, the NHS staff requesting the funds and the DHSS customer divisions considered that £3,000,000 would be well spent financing a clinical management system in one hospital which went far beyond the capabilities of any system hitherto implemented. Thirdly, it was surprising that so many members of the committee were prepared to resign over this issue when the experimental scheme to develop patient administration systems with very limited capabilities had experienced substantial difficulties.

There was then a period for licking of wounds. It ended with the DHSS setting up the NHS Computer Policy Committee (CPC) in 1981, an excellent opportunity, one would have thought, to create a national body to support the work of the Steering Group. However, the decision to appoint a regional chairman and a membership of mainly regional officers to the CPC was seen by a lot of people as civil servants distancing themselves from a NHS 'hot potato' rather than a constructive attempt to promote the coordination of NHS information services. Since the Bland report,[3] published at this time, proposed that the NHS should also assume responsibility for training, it can be surmised that civil servants had tired of criticism from the NHS and ministers about their handling of information, computing and training and were inclined to let the service make its own bed then to lie on it. It is pure speculation whether they also intended to give the NHS enough rope for a future hanging.

By the end of 1981 there were two NHS led bodies with overlapping responsibilities; the Steering Group reviewing data content but also responsible for the promotion of information technology, and the CPC concerned with management information systems. It was inevitable that these two bodies, led by strong, skilful and persuasive chairmen, would find collaboration difficult.

The Steering Group

The message from the Steering Group was the need to establish within the service the minimum data necessary for effective management. In 1980 there was little evidence that this was practicable, and its adoption by Mrs Körner was a considerable act of faith which has still not been fully recognised.

To ensure that information was used effectively, the Steering Group encouraged the development of a district computing capability. Districts were starting to implement a few single task applications on microcomputers and the group were quick to realise the ease with which these systems could be implemented and their potential for enlargement and extension. As data sets were completed the group searched for computer systems to implement them. If none existed, they promoted their development. Following successful opportunistic approaches to the Department of Trade and Industry, the maternity (see Chapter 10) and accident and emergency computer projects (see Chapter 11) were set up. The computing objective was not only to produce high quality management information, giving the user access to standard reports and the opportunity to make ad hoc enquiries, but to provide robust operational systems to take over routine repetitive tasks.

As districts became more knowledgable about IT and recognised the limitations of ad hoc computer investment, the Steering Group saw the need for issuing pragmatic guidance on the development of information services. Workshops were held which led to a series of publications about the development of a district policy,[4] organisational arrangements and manpower requirements,[5,6] and useful applications.[7]

The problems

Despite the interest and enthusiasm aroused by the Steering Group, the investment in IT to implement management information systems rose only slowly in the early

1980s. Clinical computing, however, was booming; all over the country enthusiasts were hunched over 'soft money' microcomputers. The reasons were that small clinical systems were relatively cheap, easier to justify because of their direct relevance to clinical care, and used small storage capacity because data were collected on relatively few patients.

On the other hand, management information systems such as a master patient index (130 characters per patient for 500,000 patients, for example) or a personnel system (500 characters per employee for 5,000 employees) require considerable storage capability and a frequent need for multi-user working. Although local staff have successfully specified and written dedicated microcomputer systems, few have overcome the difficulties inherent in multi-user, multi-site applications. District decisions about investment have also been complicated by a rapidly changing technology, the lack of a clear growth path and a scarcity of people who combine the required technical skills with a knowledge of clinical and management practice and behaviour.

As a result, districts in most regions have been faced, for most of the time, with only two computing options. Either they relied upon the regional computing centre to provide the more sophisticated systems (a time-wasting procedure) or they increased locally developed stand-alone systems to the point where they ceased to be cost-effective. Over-long development times and a lack of discussion between users and suppliers led to the development of inappropriate systems. Waiting for the computer centre's products has proved to be the worst buy in most regions.

Similar problems faced the Computer Policy Committee. They inherited responsibility for managing and developing the national standard mainframe computing systems which, although improving technically with the enhancement of an on-line facility, were becoming increasingly irrelevant to the information needs of the service. At the same time a growing number of small systems were being developed to deliver those parts of Körner which were amenable to low cost systems, including the DHSS sponsored management information project at Bromsgrove and Redditch which started in late 1983. The CPC did not have the advantage of the flexible pragmatic approach adopted by the Steering Group. Under the close scrutiny of the Treasury and Public Accounts Committee its obligation was towards standardisation. It is regrettable, and probably unnecessary, that all attempts to achieve standardisation have been through the development of large mainframe systems developed by regional centres of responsibility.

Conclusion

The Steering Group anticipated the implementation of the Griffiths report[1] and the current moves to a management style which depends on information. The group's remit was to review information systems and the principles and procedures to guide their future development. For this to be achieved successfully there had to be substantial national support to provide the information technology required. The arrangements made in the early 1980s were unsuitable and set up for political ends rather than managerial needs. In order to implement the group's recommendations effectively, arrangements must be made that do not conspire to defeat the best efforts of the districts.

While the management board sets up the new structures to replace the Steering Group and CPC, they would be well advised to ponder the lessons to be learnt from the events of the last five years. They would be mistaken to assume that the Steering Group's close relationship with the service can be sustained without continuous effort, or that this relationship is unnecessary in the post-Griffiths authoritarian climate. Mrs Körner's great contribution to the development of IT was to discern as a prime objective the production of credible information for managers and clinicians; and it is this objective that determines the technology required. To ignore the primacy of the user would be disastrous.

REFERENCES

1 Department of Health and Social Security. NHS management inquiry. (Leader, Mr Roy Griffiths.) London, DHSS, 1983.
2 Department of Health and Social Security. Management services: information requirements of the health services. Health Notice HN(79)21. DHSS, 1979.
3 Department of Health and Social Security. Review Group on the National Training Council and National Staff Committees. (Chairman, C Bland.) London, DHSS, 1981.
4 Department of Health and Social Security. Steering Group on Health Services Information. Developing a district IT policy. London, King's Fund, 1983.
5 Department of Health and Social Security. Steering Group on Health Services Information. Converting data into information. London, King's Fund, 1982.
6 Department of Health and Social Security. Steering Group on Health Services Information. Making data credible. London, King's Fund, 1984.
7 Department of Health and Social Security. Steering Group on Health Services Information. Introducing IT in the district office. London, King's Fund, 1983.

6

Data protection and confidentiality

David Kenny

It is crucial to the feelings of mutual trust between patient and doctor, so vital in successful health care, that the patient can speak freely without being concerned about lack of privacy. Trust must also exist between an employer and his staff, and the NHS, the largest employer in Europe, holds a considerable amount of personal information about the people who work for it.

Although standards of confidentiality of both patient and staff data in the NHS have generally been sound, experience and some recent research have shown the need for a general review. The scrutiny of the data environment brought about by the initial studies of the Steering Group set a new tone in tackling these problems and it was natural that the next step should be to set up a confidentiality working group to review the integrity and reliability of the data environment.

Past events

Over the last two decades there has been an increasing interest in issues of privacy, stimulated in the main by the growing use of computers. As long ago as 1961 an attempt was made to introduce a bill in the House of Lords. Others have since been introduced, all of them private members' bills. None has reached the statute book.

In February 1970, the Government appointed the Younger Committee 'to consider whether legislation is needed to give further protection to the individual citizen and to commercial and industrial interests against intrusions into privacy by persons and organisations, or by companies, and to make recommendations'. The committee, reporting in 1972, set out certain principles with regard to computer privacy which were intended as general guidelines to computer users in the private sector.[1]

In 1975, the White Paper, 'Computers and Privacy' and its supplement, 'Computers: Safeguards for Privacy',[2] revealed government plans to prepare legislation setting out the standards governing the use of computers which process personal information. It also proposed the establishment of a statutory data protection authority to oversee the question of privacy and computers. The Data Protection Committee under the chairmanship of Sir Norman Lindop was then appointed to advise on the legislation. It broadly endorsed the general principles set out in the Younger report.[3]

In April 1982 the Government announced in another White Paper[4] its intention to embody in legislation the principles set out in the Younger and Lindop reports.

This measured, almost laissez-faire approach, is typical of most European governments. They have done their best to limit their involvement and let events unfold rather than determine the pace of change themselves. What distinguished the UK was its low starting point; hitherto it has had no privacy legislation. The Data Protection Bill was introduced into Parliament in 1982, fell because of the general election in June 1983, was reintroduced later in 1983, and received Royal assent in June 1984. Under the Act, which is only concerned with automatically processed data, users of computer systems holding identifiable information are required to register their systems and their uses. The public register is to be controlled by an independent registrar.

The health environment

Health care presents particular problems for data protection and confidentiality, not least the general lack of clarity about the principles involved. Health care concerns a widening circle of professional, technical and support staff. Patient data are generated and retained in a great many locations in a hospital and handled at different stages by a wide range of people. There is no single patient's record, but a network of information which varies from place to place and has significant implications for anyone trying to control its dissemination.

Patients attending a hospital out-patient clinic, for example, may come into contact with a wide range of hospital staff, see Table 2, page 50. All will have legitimate access to some information about the patients, if only that they have attended the hospital. Furthermore, an increasing number of patients are now being treated in the community. Their

David Kenny

data may be handled by a variety of professional and support staff in health centres, clinics, general practitioner surgeries, and in the patients' homes. The emphasis on transferring hospital patients from institutional to community care means that patient data are transferred too, and confidentiality has to be maintained.

Table 2: Staff involved with an attendance at an out-patient clinic

a. Out-patient appointments clerk
b. Out-patient registration clerk
c. Porter/orderly in clinic
d. Out-patient clinic sister and nurses
e. Consultant and medical members of the team
f. Laboratory clerk
g. Laboratory technician
h. X-ray clerk
i. Radiographer
j. Radiologists
k. Medical secretary
l. Medical records clerks
m. Volunteer helpers

It is not only the practice of health care that complicates the maintenance of confidentiality; there is also an increasing number of external pressures which, although by and large the legitimate activities of a welfare-conscious state, present potential dangers to confidentiality. Information may be disclosed by a health professional to, among other agencies, government departments, the courts and local authority departments.

The working group's approach

Given this background it seemed to members of the Confidentiality Working Group that it was important to obtain a clear and up-to-date picture of just what was happening.

50

We therefore set up a number of studies, including:

i. a survey of the confidentiality policies in the 206 health authorities in England carried out in April 1982;
ii. a survey of policies on data destruction carried out in 24 health districts in December 1982;
iii. a detailed study of patient data traffic in 6 health districts carried out in June 1983; and
iv. a survey carried out in December 1982 of local authority social services departments' confidentiality policies.

We also made other inquiries, including a literature search and several studies in depth of individual health authorities' codes of practice for protecting data and maintaining confidentiality, in order to identify current weaknesses as well as good practices.

About the same time that the Confidentiality Working Group was set up, the BMA convened a multidisciplinary group, the Interprofessional Working Group (IPG), chaired by Sir Douglas Black. The tasks of both groups were complementary. The IPG had the responsibility for recommending ethical standards of confidentiality for health data, resolving, when necessary, differences between the health professions. The Confidentiality Working Group was responsible for reviewing the administrative policies and mechanisms used to maintain standards and recommending suitable procedures. When we identified conflicting or incomplete ethical guidance on confidentiality, we brought it, with our suggestions for remedies, to the attention of the IPG; and the IPG referred the organisational aspects of issues to us. Ideas from both groups were transmitted to the DHSS and Home Office to assist them in their work on the Data Protection Act. The DHSS have now issued for consultation a code on disclosure of personal health data.[5] This document was prepared in close collaboration with the IPG and our working group and a definitive code should be available in 1985. The Steering Group published our report[6] about the protection and maintenance of the confidentiality of patient and employee data in October 1984.

What is happening

The picture that emerged was consistent. Many health authorities do not have clear rules about who should have access to patient data and under what conditions, nor how confidentiality standards should be achieved. Our survey of district health authorities showed that less than a third of those who replied had adopted or inherited a policy on data protection. Staff guidance on the maintenance of confidentiality was often little more than a brief talk about its importance during professional training or as part of an induction course.

There is, however, a considerable volume of requests for access to patient data. Our data traffic study was carried out in the medical records departments of six districts, all of whom had a district policy about the confidentiality of patient data. During the one month period of the study there were 1,273 requests for access to data held in medical records, an average of 53 requests per week per district. The type of patient consent obtained for the release of data from medical records is shown in Table 3 (page 53), the type of doctor consent in Table 4 (page 54).

Our investigations revealed that many NHS staff are uneasy about the lack of clarity concerning issues of confidentiality and about ways of ensuring that patient data are kept secure. The survey of health authorities' confidentiality practices showed that some staff are not aware of the standards of confidentiality expected of them – particularly the need to obtain patient consent for certain types of disclosures – and of their obligation to achieve these standards. Gossip and careless talk by staff can lead to breaches of confidentiality which could be avoided by proper training.

There were also instances of current guidance about access to patient data being incomplete, unclear or inconsistent. The problem areas were access to identifiable data by social work departments, the police, researchers and health service managers.

It is instructive to focus upon some of the sensitive issues. For instance, we found little disagreement that it is

Table 3: The release of patient data from medical records. Type of patient consent obtained

Study done in medical records departments in six health authorities over a one month period in 1983, during which time 1273 requests for access were received.

			Type of patient consent obtained		
Source of request	Total requests made	*Not sought %	Specific consent obtained		Consent sought: no reply %
			written %	oral %	
Doctors outside the hospitals	436	72	5	0	23
DHSS	314	60	1	1	38
Non-medical representative	144	57	24	2	1
Voluntary bodies	100	43	24	19	14
Government other than DHSS	89	37	19	1	43
Insurance companies	35	40	51	0	9
Patient	34	26	26	48	0
Relatives or friends	32	53	6	9	32
Local authorities	30	77	0	0	23
Researchers	20	25	0	5	70
Other sources	39	43	11	3	43
All requests made	1273	59	10	4	27

*Consent implied in the request

essential for social workers who are part of the health care team to have access to hospital clinical data to enable them to carry out their work with individual clients and to be part of a multi-disciplinary team. The confidentiality of health data obtained by social workers must be maintained, however, as must social services information added to health records.

Until the Interprofessional Working Group was formed, the only guidance about the disclosure of identifiable patient data to the police was contained in a joint statement made in July 1980 by the BMA and the Association of Chief Constables. This document had no official standing and many doctors have pointed out that it failed to tackle the problems of police access to patient data.

In the draft code on disclosure issued by the DHSS, it is stated that disclosures may only be made to the police when they are necessary for the prevention, detection or prosecu-

Table 4: The release of patient data from medical records. Type of doctor consent obtained

Study done in medical records departments in six health authorities over a one month period in 1983. Only 1211 of the requests for data were codable for this item.

Source of request	Total requests made	*Not sought %	Specific consent obtained written %	Specific consent obtained oral %	Consent not given %
Doctors outside the hospitals	422	60	20.5	19	0.5
DHSS	289	81	13	6	0
Non-medical representative	138	72	14	4	0
Voluntary bodies	98	95	5	0	0
Government other than DHSS	89	65	24	9	2
Insurance companies	32	54	34	12	0
Patient	34	67	18	9	6
Relatives or friends	27	63	11	15	11
Local authorities	28	78	7	11	4
Researchers	19	26	69	5	0
Other sources	35	72	14	11	3
All requests analysed	1211	70	17	12	1

*Covered by agreed policies

tion of a crime which is so serious that the public interest must prevail over the individual's right to confidentiality. All requests from the police must be made to a specified person. The decision to make a disclosure must remain with the professionally qualified person who is responsible at that time for the patient's continuing care. Exceptionally, if the person is absent and the case is urgent, the decision can be made by another professionally qualified person authorised to make it in his place.

This is a difficult area. First, it is in the arena of social policy and the judgements that have to be made are more than clinical. Secondly, the doctor may not always be the best person to control the release of data – there have been examples of incautious release. Requests from the police are frequently urgent and vigorous. Arrangements for handling them must be clear to all staff, and the preferred approach would be to establish a procedure where management and clinicians jointly consider requests and make the outcome of their deliberations known to the health authority.

Until recently the advice about the conditions under which researchers may have access to identifiable patient data has been conflicting. Under the draft code issued by DHSS, researchers may have access to identifiable patient data without the explicit consent of the patient when this disclosure has been authorised by an appropriate ethical committee. Authorisation will only be forthcoming if there are safeguards to ensure that no damage or distress will be caused to the subject of the data and that the individual's anonymity in published results is secure. In practice, individual consultants in most districts currently maintain the right to decide about the disclosure of identifiable data for research purposes.

There is at present no guidance about what management functions make it necessary to have access to personal health data without the patient's consent. Consideration needs to be given to the use of identifiable data for purposes relating to the subject of the data, as well as for the production of statistics. To carry out essential health service functions managers require access to identifiable health data in some very rare instances. These can include, for example, investigating a complaint or untoward incident, responding to a claim for compensation or notice of proceedings, and investigating an allegation against a member of staff concerning patient care and treatment. Furthermore, health authority members may require access to identifiable patient data if they are members of an inquiry.

Conclusion

This is not the occasion upon which to recite the working group's recommendations. It would be out of tune with our approach because the Confidentiality Working Group report is not definitive, and thus not prescriptive. It is a snapshot of what is happening in a changing complex environment. We had hoped that time and resources would have allowed the recommendations to be tried out in one or two pilot districts on the lines of the earlier Steering Group work on data sets. Circumstances made this impossible, not want of effort. Whether the next steps will be on these lines or whether health authorities will go it alone remains to be seen.

The working group has shown that problems of confidentiality can be tackled in a sensible pragmatic way and that solutions to them can be found. The benefits of its work should be quickly realised as health authorities, managers and clinicians address themselves to these important issues in the light of the Data Protection Act.

REFERENCES

1 Home Office. Report of the Committee on Privacy. (Chairman, Rt Hon K Younger.) Cmnd 5012. London, HMSO, 1972.
2 Home Office. Computers and privacy. Computers: safeguards for privacy. Cmnd 6353 and 6354. London, HMSO, 1975.
3 Home Office. Report of the committee on data protection. (Chairman, Sir Norman Lindop.) Cmnd 7341. London, HMSO, 1978.
4 Home Office. Data Protection: the Government's proposals for legislation. Cmnd 8539. London, HMSO, 1982.
5 Department of Health and Social Security. Confidentiality of personal health information. Letter. DA(84)25. DHSS, 1984.
6 Department of Health and Social Security. Steering Group on Health Services Information. The protection and maintenance of confidentiality of patient and employee data: a report from the Confidentiality Working Group. (Chairman, Mrs E Körner.) London, DHSS, 1984.

7

Financial information

Trevor Rippington

There is a story which accountants like to tell against themselves. A balloonist loses his way and is forced to come down in a field in a strange neighbourhood. Fortunately, a man is just passing and the balloonist asks where he is. 'Ah yes', says the man, 'you are in a balloon which has come down in a field. You are standing in the basket facing north and it is 9.30 am'. 'Thank you', says the balloonist, 'but tell me, are you an accountant?'. 'Yes, but how did you guess?' replies the man. 'Well', says the balloonist, 'your information is absolutely accurate but totally useless.'

In defence of the accountant, it must be said that being able to provide useful information depends on having the right data and an effective way to process them. Hence in the past, in the public and the private sectors, financial information has tended to consist of that which is easiest to produce and for which there is the greatest demand.

Historical perspective

One of the earliest shocks suffered by the National Health Service was that it was costing very much more than anticipated. Consequently in 1950 the Ministry of Health called upon authorities to provide it with estimates of expenditure under a number of significant headings, and to produce monthly statements of expenditure in order to avoid overspendings. The limited information then available about activity levels in the service and the crude methods used for analysing expenditure meant the natural thing to ask for was a subjective analysis breaking down expenditure under pay and non-pay headings. This system continued until 1974 as the main means by which regional hospital boards monitored hospital management committees and the Department of Health monitored the boards.

By 1956 it had become clear that this monitoring system alone was insufficient to ensure effective financial control. That year the Guillebaud Committee on the cost of the National Health Service said in its report about financial control:

We are convinced that the present system of relying entirely on subjective costing is unsatisfactory because it fails to reveal to the heads of hospital departments how the annual expenditure of their departments varies in time and space. . . . It is at the unit level where economies can be effected and it is essential that all hospitals should have a system of accounts which will make their budgetary control effective.[1]

The committee went on:

We appreciate that hospital costs alone do not necessarily reflect the efficiency of hospital management and that they are better examined with other statistical indices such as bed occupancy, length of stay of patients, bed turnover, turnover interval, waiting time, staffing ratios, etc. It is one of the problems of management – and a particularly difficult one in the case of the hospital service – to find the right indices for measuring efficiency.

The result, in 1957, was the introduction of a national system of hospital costing at first for the larger acute hospitals only, but, ten years later, for all hospitals. The new system broke down expenditure by departments and related it to statistics of work load. From 1957, the two systems of control continued with costing taking a poor second place to the monitoring of expenditure. It has to be admitted that management generally did not take the results of costing exercises very seriously, and the reasons are not hard to find. The non-financial information was often unreliable, staffing resources were rarely adequate and much of the information, such as the cost of in-patients, was too broad for effective use.

During the late 1960s and early 1970s, a number of significant developments took place: the work of Feldstein[2] on the implications of specialty mix; the development of hospital activity analysis; the introduction of financial and statistical computer systems; the development of functional management in service departments with experiments in budgetary control; and the introduction of planning, programming, budgeting (PPB) techniques in the public service.

By the early 1970s, it had become clear that financial information had to cover three main areas: the financial control systems needed to be integrated with the costing analysis to make the departmental analysis the prime requirement;[3] the PPB approach required developing so that financial information could be linked to service objectives and analysed accordingly (that is, by care groups such as the aged, the mentally ill); and a further analysis of hospital costs was needed by specialty. The 1974 reorganisation was an opportunity to revise the national financial system in an attempt to meet all these requirements. The new system that emerged provided financial accounts that were based mainly on functional headings with subjective breakdowns as a sub-analysis. Cost accounts were to follow the same lines, thus achieving a single system. It was hoped to extend the analysis to cover a specialty breakdown.

During the 1970s further developments took place. Of particular significance was the investigation by Iden Wickings of clinical budgeting procedures, giving clinicians a direct interest in the cost control of all the activities directly affected by their decisions. David Owen pointed out that the average clinician generated expenditure of £250,000 per year[4] so that the potential for saving by making the financial consequences of his activities more explicit was substantial. Of equal importance was the development of specialty costing in Cardiff under Professor Magee. In the early 1980s it was extended to seven other centres. The development of a statistical breakdown of specialty costs was carried out by Professor Ashford at Exeter University. Meanwhile, in the United States work on the significance of case mix and costs based on the pioneering study of Fetter at Yale was being introduced into government financing systems for Medicare patients.

PPB developments suffered from too rigid an approach and interest had died in the public sector by the late 1970s.[5] However, the need for broad information about the client groups identified in the planning systems in the NHS had led to the development of ad hoc systems.

With the widespread introduction in the 1980s of computerised patient administration systems, the availability of local computing facilities and a recognition of the need for tighter management at all levels in the service, the scene was set for the Steering Group's work on finance information.

The general approach

In the past, central government has made little use of the mass of information returned to it, although the subjective analysis of expenditure has been widely used for price adjustments to financial allocations and has enabled the DHSS to convince the Treasury that a separate health service index is essential. The central publication of information about NHS spending has usually been inadequate and too late for effective action to be taken. Despite exhortations by the Secretary of State, little interest has been aroused by the annual costing summaries; the summarised financial accounts have been criticised in the Committee of Public Accounts as being out-dated and uninformative.

The major influence in the development of NHS financial systems has generally been the need for central government to exercise financial control. Information has usually moved upwards, from unit to district to region to the Department. Yet as long ago as 1956 the Guillebaud committee had recognised that it is at unit level where economies can best be effected and that the information provided at local level should be the most appropriate for local needs, not the best fitted for a nationally determined format.

The Steering Group recognised this fundamental problem in the sixth report and stated 'we believe that our proposals strike the right balance between the need for local freedom and for national prescription'.[6] A series of minimum data sets should be routinely collected to provide, at reasonable cost, the basic information required by authorities and their officers to fulfil their responsibilities. Information not required for operational use or for the districts' own purposes will not normally be required regionally or nationally. The reliability and timeliness of data improve if they are collected as a by-product of operational procedures.

The outstanding merit of each of the reports by the Steering Group is the way fundamental objectives have been carefully considered and assessed before recommendations have been made. The sixth report describes the first comprehensive financial system designed on this basis. It carefully analyses what the system should comprise, setting out the four fundamental questions that need to be answered, namely:

What is the money spent on?
Who spends the money?
Where is the money spent?
Why is it spent?

The answers suggest a need for a *subjective* analysis indicating what the money is spent on; a *budgetary* analysis showing who is responsible; a *location* analysis for where the money is spent; and a *departmental* analysis showing why money is spent as an intermediate step leading eventually to a *patient care* analysis.

The subjective analysis presents little difficulty. Its main value is at national level so it is reasonable to have a national classification. Similarly there should be a national coding structure for the location analysis. Budgetary control, on the other hand, requires an analysis which fits in with the local management pattern. This is affected by matters such as the size, location and type of hospital which cannot be determined centrally. For this reason, the Steering Group confined themselves to setting out a recommended code of practice.

The main debate in the sixth report centres on the need for patient care analysis. The group state:

We believe that the absence of a uniform generally available cost analysis of different kinds of patient care in hospital and community services by patient group characteristics (eg. age, diagnosis, specialty) severely limits the ability of districts to manage, and adversely affects planning, monitoring and performance evaluation at all levels.

The main options for producing this type of information are shown in Table 5.

Table 5: Main options for patient care analysis

1 *Patient costing*
A cost is produced for every patient treated.

2 *Diagnostic group costing*
An average cost is produced for treating patients with the same disease or with diseases falling within a defined diagnostic category.

3 *Clinical team costing*
An average cost is identified for patients treated by a particular clinician or clinical team.

4 *Specialty costing*
An average cost is identified for patients treated by clinicians working in the same specialty or group of specialties.

5 *Client group costing*
An average cost is identified for treating patients with certain broad common characteristics (for example the old, the mentally ill).

As the report indicates, the resources required to introduce refined types of costing are considerable. To accomplish the degree of accuracy required could be difficult unless there are clear incentives to do so. The Steering Group, therefore, recommend that the most commonly used and structurally developed form of costing – specialty costing – be introduced on a mandatory basis. While there may be some variation in exact methods, a minimum requirement is specified. For activities unsuitable for specialty costing, mainly the work done in community services, programme costing is recommended. The report recognises, however, that further research and development are required and encourages authorities to experiment with more refined systems, including patient costing.

The report is backed up by a clear summary of recommendations and contains appendices setting out the minimum data sets. Further work is being undertaken on the detailed work units, which will be derived from the minimum data sets recommended in the other reports, to supplement the Steering Group's recommendations. On one aspect the group were able to offer only interim guidance. This concerns capital, and the group decided to wait for the results of the review of asset and capital accounting being carried out by the Association of Health Service Treasurers.

The future

The Griffiths report,[7] now being implemented, recommended that certain aspects of business management budgets be introduced into the NHS. They were to involve managers, including clinicians, responsible for incurring costs. The ministerial review process, whereby ministers meet with regional health authority chairmen to review progress on plans and set targets, is now established, and RHA chairmen similarly meet their counterparts in district authorities. It is proposed that this process be extended to units. A further tightening of the accountability process has been the requirement that short-term programmes show how expenditure plans are related to work load estimates.

These changes make the sixth report relevant and timely. The increased emphasis on accountability to the Secretary of State does not call for a greater quantity of information, but more relevant and coordinated information. While the need for more business-like management at unit level requires the production of early, simple and relevant facts about spending related to work-load.

Specialty costing provides the basis for management

budgets and the Secretary of State has recognised this by laying the main responsibility for the pilot schemes on the 'Magee' centres for specialty costing. The need to develop methods of assessing work-load which will be acceptable to clinicians has led to research being undertaken in the UK to refine the concept of diagnostic related groups now used extensively in the United States. There is also interest in techniques like indices of severity of disease on admission.

Future developments rely on good data processing facilities being available. The hardware presents no problem, except for choice. Software is another matter and activities need to be concentrated on its development. Lessons can be learned from the group's approach; it coordinated local and national needs on the principle that information not required for districts' own purposes will not normally be required regionally or nationally.

The requirements of financial systems in the NHS are dependent on managerial and political needs. The sixth report sits logically within this pattern. If its message is followed, the balloonist's dilemma will not be shared by the NHS.

REFERENCES

1 Committee of enquiry into the cost of the National Health Service. Report. (Chairman, C W Guillebaud.) Cmd 9663. London, HMSO, 1956.
2 Feldstein M S. Economic analysis for health service efficiency. Amsterdam, North Holland, 1967.
3 Baddeley S and Tagg T A J. Better financial management in hospitals. The Hospital 1968, vol 64, no 8. 272–276.
4 Owen D. In Sickness and in Health: the politics of medicine. London, Quartet Books, 1976.
5 Van Gunsteren H R. The quest for control: a critique of the rational central planning approach in public affairs. Bristol, John Wiley, 1976.
6 Department of Health and Social Security. Steering Group on Health Services Information. Sixth Report. A report on the collection and use of financial information in the National Health Service. (Chairman, Mrs Edith Körner.) London, HMSO, 1984.
7 Department of Health and Social Security. NHS management inquiry. (Leader, Mr Roy Griffiths.) London, DHSS, 1983.

8

Manpower information

Graham Guest

The case for having a good personnel system in the NHS is overwhelming: it employs over 750,000 people in approximately 5,000 different jobs and has a wages bill of over £7,000 million. Yet, ten years ago there was nothing except a very inadequate manual statistical system processed by the DHSS, and today only the STAMP system and others like it exist. They have perpetuated many of the intrinsic management faults of the older manual system.

Problems with current systems

The national standard manpower computer system, STAMP, is simple and cheap, and adequately fulfils its specification providing the effort is made to run it. The design has limitations, however. Its prime task is to obtain the data required for central returns cheaply – mainly from payroll – and to provide authorities with limited information for local purposes. STAMP and other systems based on payroll share a number of faults. The manpower information is always considered to be less important than payroll information; consequently the data not related to payroll, such as occupation codes, are suspect. There are incompatibilities between data derived from payroll and data used for accounting purposes, and the flexibility required by district managers is lacking.

However, the worst design fault is that the logical relationship between manpower and payroll information has been lost. Payroll should depend on knowing what manpower is and has been available and these data ought to exist first in a personnel and manpower system. Payroll data would then be generated from manpower control systems not, as with STAMP, the other way round. For these and other reasons the time was ripe for the comprehensive review of manpower systems which the Steering Group dealt with in the third report to the Secretary of State.[1] It is a highly innovative document.

The Steering Group's recommendations

The minimum data set principle developed by the group is the most radical change in NHS information philosophy since the inception of the service.

> We propose the routine collection of a series of minimum data sets to provide, at reasonable cost, the basic information which district authorities need to discharge their responsibilities. Information not required for the districts' own purposes will not normally be required regionally or nationally.[1]

These revolutionary statements challenge district health authorities to manage their own manpower. No longer will central requirements dominate the development of information systems; instead the needs of districts will determine their design and operation.

The principles behind the proposals are simple. There are to be two sets of data available to authorities, one relating to posts and the other to employees. The data about posts describe the skills needed, work location, volume of work and costs. For medical and dental posts additional data are to be collected about the nature of the post. The employee set comprises personal data, position data, and data about skills, absences, costs and the dates of joining and leaving. With 5,000 different types of employee in the NHS, careful specification of each item is necessary and the report makes a first attempt to do this.

The history of NHS manpower information systems, linked as they were to central systems which have operated for many years, makes it inevitable that there will be disagreements about the central data requirement. With over 750,000 staff, or even the smaller number of 35,000 medical and dental staff, it is very unlikely that significant decisions at a national level would require figures accurate to a single individual. The reluctance of the Steering Group to accept Lord Rayner's conclusions on the maintenance of a central comprehensive medical staff index is important. It reflects the group's view that, even for medical and dental staff, it is

69

the local decisions on resource implications and need for care that are of crucial importance – even if the DHSS continues to receive information about individual employees. Some regions have already increased the quantity of information available about the use of medical manpower.

The report highlights the group's intention to relate manpower data to both workload and costs. First steps to use information derived from these three sources are now being taken in districts. These developments will rely on the existence of suitable computer systems and the report stresses the need for a new type of integrated manpower computer system. STAMP-type systems have served the NHS in the past but they are totally inadequate for the management needs of the late 1980s. The group reject systems which depend on payroll and suggest:

> A more satisfactory way of meeting the criteria would be through the introduction of a district manpower information system which would be:
> a. comprehensive;
> b. integrated with the payroll system, to feed information to it and draw information from it; and
> c. capable of being interfaced directly with the accounting system to facilitate the link with budgetary control, costing processes and financial systems.[1]

Future developments

The realisation of these integrated systems must now be a major goal of NHS computing policies. Piecemeal developments of parts of the system are taking place already and the dangers of duplicated data collection are immense – there are over 750,000 separate records on which to practice the art. An integrated system starts from the creation of a post to be filled. It then records every significant personnel and pay transaction for the individual and ends with the issuing of retirement documents. It should be linked with the payroll and accounting systems.

The way in which each region chooses to realise this goal will be different, but all will share something in common. The basic elements of database technology must be present, for example, although it would be foolish to pretend that a common database blueprint exists. History has shown just how difficult and expensive it is to achieve a fully co-ordinated computer system across the whole of the NHS. To avoid the mistakes of the past we must learn to walk before we can run and be wise enough to avoid potential disasters, like trying to integrate workload and accounting data with man-power data long before it is possible. Examples from the past counsel caution while today's economics demand swift improvements. Finding the right set of compromises will be difficult but Mrs Körner's wise and forward looking recommendations provide a sound basis for developing the information systems which will help districts control their manpower effectively.

REFERENCE

1 Department of Health and Social Security. Steering Group on Health Services Information. Third Report. A report on the collection and use of information about manpower in the National Health Service. (Chairman, Mrs Edith Körner.) London, HMSO, 1984.

9

Information about community health services

Walter Holland

To understand the current position of community health statistics and the contribution of the Steering Group, it is helpful to trace briefly the history of the public health movement in this country. From 1848 to 1974 public health was a distinct activity under the control of local public health departments. Although these departments no longer exist, the current range of community health services provided by district health authorities reflect their past efforts. Chave, in the *Oxford Textbook of Public Health*, gives a comprehensive account of the evolutionary path of public health in Britain.[1]

Historical perspective

Public health has its origins within the poor law organisations. In the late nineteenth century its importance was highlighted by the work of Edwin Chadwick who recognised the association between environmental conditions and health. The basis of his 'sanitary idea' was that disease was caused by foul air and this could be alleviated by appropriate drainage and sanitation systems. He proposed the setting up of locally based organisations to supervise the improvement of sanitation systems and to promote public health. These proposals were accepted and a series of local boards of health were established and the post of medical officer of health created as the local officer charged with preventing endemic diseases, initially cholera and typhoid.

Until the end of the nineteenth century, medical officers of health were concerned primarily with the environment, particularly housing, sanitation and infectious diseases. The revelation that large numbers of volunteers to serve in the Boer War were unsuitable on health grounds hailed a shift in the emphasis of public health services. It was evident that environmental sanitation was not enough to secure an adequate standard of health for the nation. The beginning of the twentieth century saw the implementation of a range of welfare policies, including the provision of school meals, the establishment of the school medical service to provide routine medical inspection and clinics for the treatment of minor ailments, and reform of the mid-wifery profession. From the First World War onwards, growing emphasis was placed on the provision of services for vulnerable groups, particularly pregnant women and children. All these services were organised locally through the boards of health. As methods of diagnosis and treatment became available, clinics for specific conditions such as tuberculosis and venereal diseases were established. These clinics and, in 1929, the poor law institutes including the infirmaries and municipal hospitals also came under the jurisdiction of the medical officer of health.

Following the introduction of the National Health Service in 1948, control of hospital services passed to regional hospital boards. However, medical officers of health, now employed by local authorities, retained control of a whole range of services; the scope of which continued to diversify including at one time the supervision of social workers. This was a period of dynamic innovation. Responding to local demands and perceived needs, major progress was made in developing and improving services. Examples included the building and organisation of health centres; the employment of midwives; the use of health visitors in developmental work among children and for caring for the elderly; and improvements in the coverage of services such as those for immunisation.

Medical officers of health were directly accountable to their employers, the local authorities, to whom they were required to submit regular reports; the production of which encouraged the collection of information about the services. These reports illustrate the crusading spirit of these medical officers of health and demonstrate what can be achieved when appropriate information is available.

However, there were many problems with this piecemeal development of information systems. First, and fundamentally, there was little comparability between local authorities. Even within a single area, data collected over time was not necessarily consistent. One large metropolitan area, for example, noted a fall in the height of children from one year to the next. On closer investigation it was found that in one year height was measured with shoes on and in the next without. There was an absence of standardisation of definitions. Thus, the observation from epidemiological investigations of a higher incidence of various abnormalities in poorer than richer communities was not confirmed in the annual reports of medical officers of health. Perforated ear drum appeared to be more frequent in well off areas. This discrepancy was explained by the fact that doctors practising in richer areas spent more time looking for and recording such abnormalities.

Despite the obvious flaws and the lack of standardisation, these reports represent pioneering work in the organisation and collection of information about community needs and the use of health services. However, while some authorities had already developed excellent information systems, for example for immunisation, and had demonstrated the application of such systems to improving uptake, much of the information was of minimal value as a management tool. Efforts concentrated largely on tabulating numbers with little attempt to collect data on denominators and to assess outcomes. Furthermore, information about service use was rarely linked to information about service costs.

The amalgamation of public health with hospital services in 1974 was an inevitable move intended to create an integrated health service. Although it was evident that the achievement of a truly integrated service would require a more appropriate and rationalised information system, and despite the valuable ground work that had been carried out in many local authorities, reorganisation did not bear the expected fruits in terms of innovative information systems. Instead, integration served to hold back progress in developing systems and to diminish interest. Many of the early pioneers disappeared from the scene and interest became increasingly focussed on hospital-based activities.

The Steering Group

It was amid this chaos that the Steering Group enters the story, with a remit to review information systems covering all aspects of the integrated health service.

Community services are an important resource within the health service, both to maintain and improve the community's health by complementing and, where possible, substituting for hospital care. It is essential, if the community services provided by district health authorities are to serve their appropriate role within this system, that managers have adequate information about what services are being provided and how effective they are. This information must also by linked with that about hospital activities and the activities of general practitioners, who provide a major proportion of community health services and are presently independent of NHS information systems.

The contribution of the Steering Group has been to clarify and define the activities that constitute community health services and to provide a clear framework for collecting relevant information for making meaningful assessments of their effectiveness and their resource requirements.[2]

The activities of community health services have been clearly differentiated into two categories. These are services to the community, for example, immunisation and vaccination, prevention programmes, and school health services; and secondly, health care within the community, that is, services to sick or handicapped individuals outside hospital. Within these two categories, groupings of related activities have been identified.

A framework for collecting a simplified set of data which would provide the health services manager with the minimum necessary information is proposed. For services to the community, the Steering Group approach links policy objectives, target populations, performance and costs. In this way it should be possible to assess the effectiveness and use of resources by different services. Similarly, for services providing care in the community, their objectives, catchment population, population under treatment and costs are

77

linked to allow community needs to be defined and adequately costed.

An important aspect of community health information systems is the identification of events within a population in order to fully understand the performance of the services provided. At present, such a population register is not available, although in Tayside an attempt has been made to introduce a register with appropriate linkage.[3,4] It is essential to establish a suitable population register if the full potential of the Steering Group recommendations are to be realised.

As Baldwin stated in 1972,[5] the capability of a community health system to link one event to another is crucial for defining the prevalence and incidence of disease and determining the needs for services and the appropriate scheduling of interventions, immunisations for example. The difficulties of presently available population registers for providing management information, such as that for the child health computer system, have been described by Scrivens.[6] This system is useful in collecting information on individual children and as an administrative tool for scheduling appointments and producing aggregated statistical information. However, while the system allows the collection of a variety of data about children and their parents, little thought has been given to what information to produce and for what purpose. Scrivens illustrates the potential value of such linkage of information for management purposes in answering questions such as: Which children do not attend? What are their characteristics? What changes should be made to achieve the policy objective of higher levels of immunisation uptake? Similarly by linking information from the present system with information from other sources about children who have already had measles or whose parent opted to obtain immunisation through their GP, O'Mahony[7] has demonstrated certain inadequacies of the present system.

Conclusion

The recommendations of the Steering Group represent a major step forward, in setting out an approach to providing comparable data about health care activities for and within the community. Nonetheless, it must be emphasised that the full potential of the new system as a management tool must await the realisation of an appropriate linkage with information about general practice and hospital activities and, through a population register, the facility to relate the information to a defined population group.

The work of the Steering Group is an important landmark on the way to developing appropriate health service information systems in the 20th century. It is unfortunate that it has taken so long to establish valid data collection systems but the complexities and difficulties of undertaking this task should not be underestimated. The training required in order to ensure that data are collected appropriately is enormous. Community staff already spend a large proportion of their time in recording data for operational purposes. It is important, therefore, that these data are used to provide information about the impact of interventions on the health of the population being served. It is only when managers start using such information that the underlying aim of the Steering Group will have been achieved.

REFERENCES

1 Chave S P W. The discipline of health and disease: the origins and development of public health. In: Holland W W, Detels R, Knox G, eds. Oxford textbook of public health, volume 1: History determinants, scope and strategies. Oxford, Oxford University Press, 1984. 1–19.

2 Department of Health and Social Security. Steering Group on Health Services Information. Fifth Report. A report on the collection and use of information about services for and in the community in the National Health Service. (Chairman, Mrs Edith Körner.)

3 Bodenham K E, Wellman F. Foundations for health service management. London, Oxford University Press for Nuffield Provincial Hospitals Trust, 1972.

4 Tayside Health Board. The Tayside master patient index. Dundee, Tayside Health Board, 1978.

Walter Holland

5 Baldwin J A. The role of the Community Health Information System in epidemiology and monitoring. In Symposium on community health information systems. Oxford, Department of Regius Professor of Medicine, Oxford University, 1972. 5.1–5.18.
6 Scrivens E. Management information in the National Health Service: the use of the child-health computer system. Community Medicine, 1984, vol 6, no 4. 299–305.
7 O'Mahony E. Personal communication, 1985.

10

Information about maternity care

Michael Goldacre and Frances Martin

There is a long tradition of interest in information relating to birth and the health of mothers and infants. Civil registration of births and deaths – undertaken for legal, administrative and demographic reasons as much as for medical reasons – goes back at least a century in many industrialised countries and more than two centuries in some. Both for historical and geographical comparisons, infant mortality rates and perinatal mortality rates are among the most commonly used indicators of a population's health status and social development. Such statistics as birth and fertility rates, infant and perinatal mortality rates, have thus long been the province not only of health professionals but of others concerned with measuring the growth, development and health of populations.

There is also a long tradition of clinical audit of obstetric and perinatal practice by individual clinicians, firms and hospitals. For many years it has been common for maternity hospitals to produce their own annual clinical reports. As knowledge has developed about the factors which influence perinatal mortality and morbidity, clinical and statistical reports on maternity care have increasingly included information, reported in a structured way, concerning such variables as the infant's birthweight, length of gestation, the mother's age and parity, associated clinical conditions, the method of onset of labour and method of delivery.

Other well established interests in perinatal medicine and statistics include systems to identify possible adverse effects of drugs (stimulated notably by the thalidomide incident) and infective organisms (such as rubella) in the pre-natal period; and studies concerned with the assessment of perinatal influences on medical and social outcomes in infancy, childhood and even into adult life (for example, the 1946 and 1958 British birth cohort surveys).

Current information systems

Despite the wide-ranging interest in information about maternities, coverage of births in England and Wales by maternity information systems has in some respects been fragmented, poorly coordinated and unsatisfactory. Birth certification and civil registration have been universal and invaluable, of course, but the information recorded is inadequate for the purpose of monitoring maternity care in detail. Birth notification is a statutory requirement and includes a number of items of obstetric and neonatal clinical interest; but, until the recent advent of child health computer systems, notification data were not readily available in processed form for the production of statistical information relating to large populations.

Maternity HIPE, which was developed during the 1950s, contains data from a ten per cent sample of all discharges of maternity cases but this sampling fraction means that the data are often insufficient for detailed local analysis.[1] Maternity HAA, which has been developed more recently, includes information about all discharges of maternity cases in hospitals which it covers; but, at the time when the Steering Group was undertaking its work, this system was used in fewer than 50 hospitals. HIPE and HAA include data about babies in special care baby units (SCBUs). However, neither HIPE nor HAA usually contain data about infants born in hospital who have not been admitted to SCBUs; and, even for those who have been admitted, the data relevant to the analysis of perinatal care are sparse.

In order to provide more satisfactory data than that obtainable from these sources, initiatives had been taken by the Royal College of Obstetricians and Gynaecologists (RCOG) and by the British Paediatric Association (BPA) to develop, respectively, the standard maternity information system[2] and the neonatal discharge record.[3] Both were in relatively early stages of development – and neither had achieved wide geographical coverage – when the Steering Group was formed, but both clearly had much to offer to the work of the group.

The problems and challenges

Requirements for information systems about maternity care differ from those for other specialties in a number of obvious but important respects. Firstly, the Steering Group had to consider the problem of the variety of different information systems relating to the birth event. In particular, the group recognised that the information systems being developed by the RCOG and the BPA were different from one another but presumably not, the group felt, irreconcilable. High priority was placed by the group on agreeing a common set of data which would serve the needs of obstetricians, paediatricians and general practitioners and which would, by acting as a common set, reduce the need for replicate collection of the same data for different information systems. Great credit must go to the clinicians working with the Steering Group for the willingness with which they established, early on in the group's work on maternity, that agreement could and would be reached on a set of data which would form the common core of a maternity information system to meet a number of different clinical needs.

A second point of difference between maternity and other specialties is that, in maternity, although the recording of care starts with one individual, it is usually eventually concerned with two or more. The implication of this for information systems has been neatly described by Dr Peter Dunn. 'Naturally, each mother is recognised as a patient with her own hospital number, clinical record and discharge letter. The problem is that these women behave in a way no other National Health Service patient behaves. While in hospital they give birth to another NHS patient!'[3] The Steering Group accepted (as had the proponents of the neonatal discharge record) that each infant needed to be documented in its own right. The group also accepted – and had to address the problem – that there was a need to relate information on the mother's record to that on the baby's record.

The need to link data between mother and baby records

was not the only linkage requirement which needed considering. Whilst in other hospital specialties the Steering Group has recommended that the individual episode of continuous hospital care would be the unit of statistical account, in obstetrics it is desirable to make 'the maternity' the unit of account, already recognised in the development of the standard maternity information system. This would require a means of relating information about ante-natal assessment and pre-delivery admissions to the birth admission.

It was recognised from the outset that the group would need to recommend the inclusion of more clinical and epidemiological data in the maternity data set than in the data set for other clinical specialties. This was because there are a variety of data items relating to maternal and perinatal care whose worth in the collection and analysis of maternity statistics is well established. It is probably also fair to say that although there is much variety in obstetric practice the 'product' of healthy infants and mothers, and the clinical means to these ends, are not so heterogeneous as the means and ends covered by, for example, the practice of general medicine. The implication of this is that there are certain items of clinical data which are relevant to all, or almost all, maternity patients. For these reasons it was recognised that recommendations should be made for a system which would accommodate such data items as birth weight, length of gestation, resuscitation, method of delivery, foetal presentation and Apgar score.

A final point of difference between maternity and other specialties is that, in maternity, a 'trigger' from information systems about each birth is invariably needed speedily for operational purposes to organise health activities directed to the care of the mother and infant, such as those initiated by the systems of birth notification and the initiation of a child health record.

The recommendations

Provisional recommendations were made in the first[4] and fourth reports[5] and definitive ones in the maternity supplement.[6] Notwithstanding the respects in which needs for maternity information are different, the group proposed that maternity information systems share crucial elements in common with the system developed for collecting data on patients using a hospital bed. A data set is to be collected on the mother and each baby which differs only from the general data set in that the code of the GP responsible for ante-natal care can replace that of the usual GP; and the highest level of care received by the baby should be recorded.

As the data sets for mother and baby fit so comfortably with that for all specialities, it is possible to include these records as part of an integrated patient information system. Not only will records relating to mothers' and babies' episodes of care be processed through the same system, but ante-natal admissions will be processed with those at which birth took place, and neonatal and paediatric records will be processed together.

Some data specific to maternity could not be readily accommodated in the patient information system but were being collected as part of birth notification in many districts. The group therefore recommended the minimum content of a delivery/birth notification data set which would provide the information required for notification and could be merged with the mother and baby data sets to contribute to a composite data set for the maternity.

The final component of the maternity minimum data set are two data items obtained from birth registration – the NHS number and parental occupation – which the group felt unable to recommend for general collection. Whilst recognising the potential value of these data, the group accepted that the NHS number is little used and therefore difficult to collect; and data on occupation from which social class is derived are time-consuming and difficult to collect accurately. The Registrar of Births, however, generates the NHS number and is specially trained to collect data about occupation.

To ensure that admissions occurring during the course of a pregnancy can be analysed together, the group recommended the universal introduction of a district numbering system which will also allow the analysis of records about successive pregnancies for the same mother, providing they have occurred in the same district. The group did not feel able, at the time, to recommend as mandatory the use of identification systems which would permit the linkage of records between districts or to link maternity records to any records of subsequent death of the infant or child.

The pressure to include clinical and epidemiological data was coped with by the group recommending optional clinical data sets, which should be coded and computerised if wanted locally by doctors and if recorded by them in a structured format. Three clinical options have been described – for obstetrics (compatible with the standard maternity information system), neonatal care (compatible with the neonatal discharge record) and for anaesthetists. The divide between items in the minimum and optional data sets is based on the group's criteria of desirability, feasibility and affordability. If resources permit, it is good practice to include the clinical options as part of routine data collection.

Piloting the recommendations

The provisional recommendations about the information required for registrable births, contained in the first report,[4] were piloted in seven districts. The opportunity was taken not only to test the feasibility of data collection but also to develop microcomputer systems to process the data at local level. A joint project with the NHS Computer Policy Committee was set up in 1982 and the development phase has recently been completed.

The basic hardware and software configurations chosen by the seven sites are shown in Table 6 on page 88. The systems will all carry the data sets recommended by the

Michael Goldacre and Frances Martin

Steering Group but they differ considerably in the range of operational procedures that will be available.

Table 6: Soft and hardware choices in seven districts

District	Basic hardware	Operating system and language
Bristol	Sage IV	P and PASCAL
Camberwell	DEC PDP 11/34	DEC-RSX-11M and Compiled BASIC
Newcastle	ICL DRS 20/50	DRX and COBOL
Nottingham	DEC PDP 11/23	MUMPS
Paddington	ICL DRS 20/50	DRX and CIS COBOL
Peterborough	DMS MODATA	CP/M and D BASE II
St Helen's	EQUINOX 500	MPM AND K+M BASIC

Most of the applications follow a basic pattern. Data about pregnant mothers are entered on receipt of a referral letter or at the ante-natal booking clinic. Further data are entered after delivery and after discharge. The major differences between sites are the type of personnel inputting data to the computer (midwives or clerical staff) and the range of forms, letters and other paperwork which the system provides. The NHS Computer Policy Committee has recently evaluated all the systems and a report will be available shortly.

Most of the systems have particularly noteworthy features. The application at the Bristol Maternity Hospital, for example, has a comprehensive anaesthetic data set and is run on a 'state of the art' 16 bit microcomputer. At King's College Hospital, the site of the Camberwell application, patient details are entered by midwives during the booking appointment using light pens and bar-coded questionnaires. Other sites are considering this innovative and easy form of data entry. The Newcastle system is running on two different sites in the district and, as a successor to the standard maternity information system, electronic transmission to the regional mainframe has been established.

The application at the City Hospital, Nottingham, has been developed as a module of the regional MUMPS/DEC patient administration system and thus is totally compatible with other local patient systems. The staff at St Mary's Hospital, Paddington, have developed particularly good computer validation routines and probably the widest range of outputs relieving clerical and midwifery staff of tedious form-filling.

As a result of the piloting exercise, districts have a choice of computer applications which will not only process the recommended data set but also perform a range of operational procedures. All the systems now running are still being enhanced so it is not easy to identify a 'best buy'. When considering which application best suits your district, go and look at the pilot sites and talk to the people actually using the systems before making your choice. There is no substitute for a face-to-face discussion with the users.

REFERENCES

1 Ashley J S A. The maternity hospital in-patient enquiry. In: Chalmers I, McIlwaine G, eds. Perinatal audit and surveillance. Royal College of Obstetricians and Gynaecologists, 1980. 61–78.

2 Thomson A M, Barron S L. A standard maternity information system. In: Chalmers I, McIlwaine G, eds. Perinatal audit and surveillance. Royal College of Obstetricians and Gynaecologists, 1980. 79–92.

3 Dunn P M. A standard neonatal discharge record. In: Chalmers I, McIlwaine G eds. Perinatal audit and surveillance. Royal College of Obstetricians and Gynaecologists, 1980. 93–113.

4 Department of Health and Social Security. Steering Group on Health Services Information. First Report. A report on the collection and use of information about hospital clinical activity in the National Health Service. (Chairman, Mrs Edith Körner.) London, HMSO, 1982.

5 Department of Health and Social Security. Steering Group on Health Services Information. Fourth Report. A further report on the collection and use of information about activity in hospitals and the community in the National Health Service. (Chairman, Mrs Edith Körner.) London, HMSO, 1984.

6 Department of Health and Social Security. Steering Group on Health Services Information. Supplement to the First and Fourth Reports. Maternity Services (Chairman Mrs Edith Körner). London, HMSO, 1985.

11

The CAER project: the development of a computer based information system for A and E departments

David Wilson and Janet Ousby

I t always helps when you know what you are doing. This aphorism, commonly applied to medical work, became a cornerstone of the Steering Group's philosophy in tackling the task of suggesting improvements to information systems in the NHS. Given this approach it was not surprising that they soon appreciated that the accident and emergency department is the linchpin in relationships between the community and hospital clinical services. It is the route by which most patients enter an acute hospital and more new patients are seen in this department than all other out-patient clinics combined. It quickly became obvious that it was essential to introduce a national computer-based records system which would serve to release A&E data from the restricting confines of the handwritten record.

The SH3 statistical return shows that the equivalent of 20 per cent of the population of Great Britain presents to an accident and emergency department each year. The patients are examined, treated and discharged or admitted to hospital. During the process, items of information are collected and stored in handwritten notes, in this form uesless to anyone interested in producing meaningful information. Due to the sheer volume of patients, the only figures required centrally about A&E departments are the absolute numbers of new and total attendances. No breakdown of these national totals by, for instance, age or sex, diagnosis or disposal, is available. When one considers the potential value of such a powerful source of information as the A&E database, with its diversity of patients and their problems, it seems folly not to exploit to the full this wealth of untapped data.

Recent developments

In recent years, an attempt to remedy the situation at a local level has been made at Bristol,[1] Lancaster,[2] Bangor,[3] Salford, Stourbridge, Southampton and Leeds,[4] each developing separate systems and implementing them in different ways. This kind of initiative has fulfilled a local need but the data being collected and the information produced are not comparable between sites; also, data produced in isolation have limited use. These systems, however, helped to illustrate the paucity of A&E information on a national scale and inspired the work to be described.

The main impetus for the computer-based accident and emergency records (CAER) project was derived from the Steering Group and its first report.[5] The respect achieved by the group, and its chairwoman in particular, brought about great enthusiasm for the project. The aim of the group to consult with end-users directly paralleled the concern for more A&E data voiced most strongly by the clinicians and administrators at unit and district level. The basic philosophy of the group, that information for management purposes must be yielded as a by-product of operational procedures, fitted A and E perfectly since the numbers of patients attending and the nature of the work itself demand that information be produced as a spin-off of the normal routines.

The obvious solution to the problem of better management information and better routine procedures was computerisation. Only a computer system can give the power and capacity necessary to combine both operations. To date, the vast accumulation of A&E data has lain impotent in dusty records offices and Dickensian ledgers but, with the help of the microchip, their riches will eventually be realised.

The CAER project

Endorsed by the newly established NHS Computer Policy Committee and with the whole-hearted support of the Steering Group, the CAER project was launched in the autumn of 1982. Its objective was to produce a computer-based information and administration system for A&E departments, incorporating all the recommendations made in chapter 14 of the first report to the Secretary of State.[5] Workshops were held at which the needs of the end-users were discussed by a number of people involved in A&E

work, district information units and accident prevention and health education organisations. The users' requirements were consolidated and a team of advisers suggested the optimum technical solutions for size of computer, operating system and language.

It was decided that an A&E system should be developed which could be linked with other systems in a hospital when the need arose. This meant that a microcomputer dedicated to an A&E department would suffice, and the relatively innovative step was taken of developing national software for a micro-based system. Because of the national nature of the project, no single computer hardware manufacturer could be favoured. If possible, applications software should be written to run on a range of hardware which would give individual authorities a reasonable choice of machines.

Programmers to work with microcomputers and the UNIX operating system were recruited and the services of the Yorkshire Regional Health Authority were utilised for software development. The CAER project steering committee was formed with members from the range of disciplines represented at the workshops. A user specification was agreed and submitted to the programming team. With the purchase of two types of hardware to demonstrate the portability of the software, and the nomination of three trial A&E departments to test the system in working environments, the CAER project was under way and arousing interest.

The CAER system

The software enables clerical staff to enter data into the system about all patients attending an A&E department, produces all documentation concerning attendances, and stores data for analysis. All the normal 'house-keeping' facilities are incorporated to allow the user to take security copies and archive data, to limit access to the system and to perform other routine system management tasks.

Over and above this, however, the CAER system accommodates a range of other facilities not normally available in this type of software package. It was decided at an early stage that as much flexibility as possible should be given to each individual user-site by allowing a user to redesign much of the standard package to suit local practices and requirements. For instance, the printed outputs can be redesigned, and so can the screen layouts; the amount of data collected and stored locally can be varied; and data items not already held within the data dictionary can be added. A fully comprehensive data analysis and report generator package is an integral part of the software, enabling users to select cases and analyse their data by two- or three-dimensional cross-tabulation, by listings or by reports.

None of the features mentioned (routine data entry and output, housekeeping, redesign and data analysis) requires computing or programming expertise and, provided the documentation is consulted, the system itself will take a user through all these stages. In this way, the independence of the user-site is assured and the end-users have direct control over their systems. It must be remembered, however, that this control has to be strict and the system managed locally in a properly disciplined fashion.

Although flexibility is given to the user for local implementation, no flexibility is allowed to the data definitions used in the dictionary for the standard CAER package. A user-site is required to collect the Steering Group's minimum data set. If it collects other items of information specified in the dictionary, the standard definitions in the documentation must be used. There is little point in developing a national A&E system if the data collected are not compatible from site to site. Incompatible data cannot be compared between sites and cannot be aggregated to provide the powerful database envisaged.

The system is being tested at three trial sites: Leeds General Infirmary, Hope Hospital, Salford, and Ysbyty Gwynedd, North Wales. These centres represent a range of A&E departments as far as size, location and resources are concerned, and will be used as demonstration sites for other users. It is hoped that a centre with responsibility for the further development, support and implementation of the system will be established in the first half of 1985.

Using the information

The demand for information from A&E departments is heavy, and as varied as the discipline of A&E itself. Information from the CAER system will be used in a variety of ways.

CAER makes it easy to retrieve information about individual patients so that details of previous attendances can be linked with a new episode. This facility is particularly useful when dealing with patient groups most at risk, such as the under-5s and the over-70s. The stored records can be analysed together for information which will be of benefit locally for at least two purposes – local management and clinical and epidemiological research. For example, studies of patients' arrival times and waiting times can be linked with staffing levels in the departments; the performance of new clinical staff can be monitored; trends in workload detected; and the use of resources measured. An A&E department lies between the community and other hospital departments and the study of its performance and the identification of areas of acute activity are extremely important. Clinical and epidemiological uses are as wide-ranging and varied as the research interests. Those systems already functioning have shown the value of local data in studying the management of patient groups and patterns of illness or injury in the community.

If a number of A&E departments employ the same kind of system and collect data using the same criteria and definitions, the results can be aggregated for use regionally and nationally. The few units able to supply data have had many requests for them but the data cannot be said to truly represent the work of all A&E departments. This will be rectified once a network of departments all producing similar data, is set up around Great Britain.

Other parties outside the NHS are keen to have access to a reliable database, including the Child Accident Prevention

Trust (CAPT), the Home Accident Surveillance System (HASS), the Transport and Road Research Laboratory (TRRL), the Sports Council and the Health and Safety Executive (HSE), besides local government, some sectors of industry and commerce and other national bodies. A network of A&E departments could be invited to participate in special, coordinated studies to provide information not normally produced during the registration procedure.

Conclusion

In the last ten years, the DHSS has invested money in accident and emergency services and has brought about an improvement in senior medical staffing. Accident and emergency medicine is now an established specialty in the NHS and its status has been confirmed by the introduction of a senior registrar training programme. It is widely accepted that these changes have significantly improved the emergency care of the acutely ill and injured. The next step in developing A&E services must be a computer-based record system which will enable clinicians and administrators to improve their efficiency and economy. The CAER system will be established throughout the country during the next three years and doubtless the next generation will look back and see its introduction as the turning point in the development of information for emergency health care. The mists of 'mediaeval' statistical ignorance will finally have been dispersed.

REFERENCES

1 Mason A A. Accident records on computer. Health and Social Services Journal, 1975, vol 85. 708–709.
2 Roberts J M, Farrer J A, Harvey P W. The use of a computer system in the study of the attendance profile in a district hospital casualty department. Computers in Biology and Medicine, 1977, vol 7, no 4. 291–299.
3 Clarkson D, Gray R, Jones D, Smith P, Jones I. Microcomputer system in an accident unit. British Medical Journal, 1982, vol 284. 722–724.
4 Wilson D H. The development of accident and emergency medicine. Community Medicine 1980, vol 2. 28–35.

5 Department of Health and Social Security. Steering Group on Health Services Information. First Report. A report on the collection and use of information about hospital clinical activity in the National Health Service. (Chairman, Mrs Edith Körner.) London, HMSO, 1982.

12

Nationally available information about hospital discharges

Michael Alderson and John Ashley

For over 100 years it has been recognised that mortality statistics are a very inadequate source of data about the prevalence of disease in a community. Because there are many conditions which are not fatal or have relatively high survival rates, other statistics are required to illustrate the distribution of diseases in a population. At one time it was thought that population surveys or the registration of diseases might provide the answer, but collecting sufficient detail to verify a diagnosis is expensive and, consequently, general health surveys are seldom carried out.

Activity in the registration of chronic diseases has been limited. It has been done for cancer and there have been a few schemes for registering patients with specific rare conditions.[1] Research projects have also been carried out to detect all patients developing ischaemic heart disease in a defined community.[2] Records from general practice are another source of information about disease in the community but they have not been developed to the point where regular material is available for the country as a whole.[3]

Statistics about patients discharged from hospital, although collected primarily for clinical, management or planning purposes, have traditionally been considered a major source of information about appreciable morbidity in the community (that is, diseases of sufficient severity to warrant a spell in hospital).

The use of statistics from the Hospital In-Patient Enquiry

For many years data have been available about hospital discharges giving the diagnosis for each patient, together with demographic characteristics like date of birth, sex and locality of residence. Statistics derived from these data examine the traditional axes of persons affected, place of occurrence, and trends in the frequency of a particular condition. The following examples indicate how national statistics from the 10 per cent sample of hospital discharges, the Hospital In-Patient Enquiry (HIPE), have been utilised for epidemiological studies.

Lee[4] used the statistics from HIPE for 1956–57 to examine discharges from appendicitis. These data showed a major difference in the discharges for females compared with males. Though both sexes had an age peak in late childhood and early adolescence, the peak was much more marked in females and the level appreciably higher. This difference between the sexes applied to both immediate and other admissions.

Barker and Donnan[5] used data from HIPE for four years between 1968 and 1973 to examine the regional pattern of discharge rates for upper urinary tract stone and renal colic in England and Wales. The rates for stone and colic were combined and emergency admissions were distinguished from planned ones. It was considered that this removed some of the bias due to repeat admissions and variations in diagnostic and coding practice. They concluded that Wales and the southern regions of England had a generally higher incidence of the two conditions than northern regions. It is noteworthy that these authors felt that the data were of sufficient quality to use the term incidence rather than prevalence of admissions to hospital.

Coggan et al[6] utilised HIPE data for 1958–77 to examine the trends in discharge rates for peptic ulcer. Statistics were examined separately for men and women, for duodenal and gastric ulcer, and for whether perforation was or was not reported. Though the overall discharge rates had fallen in the 20 year period, the authors noted that there was wide variation in the trends for particular subgroups. For example, perforated ulcers became less common in young adults, whilst perforated duodenal ulcers became more common in middle-aged and elderly women.

Fraser et al[7] examined the pattern of diseases associated with hospital discharges for 1968–78, reviewing data for the 17 broad chapters of the International Classification of Diseases, and specific conditions within these broad headings. They acknowledged that discharge rates result as a complex interaction between morbidity, bed supply, social circumstances, the referral pattern of general practitioners and consultants' decisions on the appropriateness of admission. Allowing for these, the data on discharge were thought to prove useful in considering the changing pattern of disease in the community.

Specific conditions that have been explored using HIPE statistics include Paget's disease and its relationship with Vitamin D deficiency;[8] cerebrovascular disease and the consideration of diet and associated factors;[9] the geographical differences in the prevalence of chronic bronchitis;[10] the seasonal variation and time trends in childhood asthma;[11] and trends in self-poisoning.[12]

The difficulties of interpreting hospital discharge statistics have been considered by a number of authors.[13,14] A particular problem is the validity of the discharge diagnosis, which is a data item of crucial epidemiological importance. Attention always needs to be given to the degree to which there is selection bias for admission (are some subgroups in the population more likely to be admitted, independent of the severity of their condition?); the problem of repeat admissions and the inability to identify a count of subjects with a given disease; and the relevance of a discharge diagnosis as a marker of morbidity in the community. Because of the difficulty in distinguishing repeat admissions by one person from single admissions by many individuals, Acheson[15] established the Oxford Record Linkage Study in 1962. Though this project continues, there is no possibility of linking repeat admissions at national level in England and Wales and future statistics will continue to be event based (that is derived from counts of discharges which do not distinguish the numbers of individuals involved).

Problems with the current information systems

At the time the Steering Group was formed, the statistical systems covering what was then referred to as hospital in-patients were overdue for a major overhaul. There were signs of incoordination and a considerable degree of duplication.

The annual hospital return (SH3) has provided basic

secular trends by individual hospital over a period of more than 30 years but the limitations in the use of the data have become increasingly unacceptable: it is not always compatible with the classification used in the statistics of medical manpower; measures of performance on SH3 are restricted to the number of discharges and day cases, and to simple information about throughput and length of stay; and although these statistical returns have been completed in most hospitals with great care, there has not always been strict adherence to all the requisite definitions.

It was hoped that the deficiencies of the crude measures of activity represented on SH3 might have been offset by the increasing use of hospital activity analysis (HAA) and HIPE, which in recent years has been derived from HAA. However, HAA has not fulfilled its initial expectations. Undoubtedly it has contributed to a variety of applications and assisted in a better understanding of many problems but, by and large, its critics have been more vociferous than its advocates. Particular complaints have been made about unsatisfactory timeliness, completeness and accuracy. Most regional health authorities have centrally processed paper based systems with slow procedures for data acquisition, validation and correction. Incompleteness has often been due to the local problems of data acquisition associated with paper based, clerically controlled systems. Output is delayed by the slow process of assembling an edited file and then analysing it. Much of the criticism of accuracy has been directed at the standards of coding of the clinical information, although research studies such as that by Martini et al[16] have shown that the diagnostic data are only 'as good as the clinical notes on which they have been based'.

As well as the general HAA/HIPE systems, there is a variety of maternity systems and the Mental Health Enquiry (MHE) for psychiatric patients. MHE was set up to be complementary to regular censuses of mental hospital beds and was designed to allow person-based information to be generated, although this facility has not often been used. The autonomous nature of the MHE means that different data sources have to be consulted if comparisons are required between, for example, long-stay psychiatric patients and long-stay geriatric patients.

Nationally the collection of maternity information has been different from that for other specialties. Much of the input is on clerically completed forms whereas the general HIPE system is on magnetic tapes derived from the existing regional HAA computer systems. The clerical extraction of the basic data has not usually involved the regional quality control teams responsible for standards in HAA. The timeliness of data production has also been poor.

The Steering Group's recommendations

These covered five basic areas: the improvement of definitions and classifications; the tightening of coordination between the various systems; the concept of a district spell; guidance about the timeliness and availability of information; and, most important, changes of attitude to information. It was clear that there are many instances where definitions have become outdated or are no longer related to modern clinical practice; some classifications, such as that for operative procedures, need thorough revision. The Steering Group recognised that if information is to be generally used it must be credible and great pains were taken to ensure that the new data reflect current methods of clinical care.

It is no longer tenable to have three separate systems for different aspects of hospital care and it makes good sense to incorporate maternity and psychiatry. Recognising that hospital utilisation data are required for epidemiological as well as health management purposes requires the linkage of separate episodes of hospital care in a person rather than an episode oriented system. Present practice frequently involves patients in episodes of care in more than one institution during a continuous spell in hospital. The concept of a district spell and the introduction of a district numbering system as proposed in the first report[17] will facilitate the linking of episodes into spells and the linking of spells in the same district.

The most important part of the group's work has been to generate debate and discussion on a wide range of topics about the provision and dissemination of information. Stimulating a positive approach to information matters will do more to improve standards of information than cosmetic surgery to the detail, timely though that is. Practical proposals have been made to encourage the development of local information systems in district health authorities.[18,19] If they ensure that full use is made of the data collected, an improvement in validity will follow.

Implementation

The Steering Group's recommendations about hospital discharge data will be implemented by April 1987, apart from birth and delivery information which will be introduced one year later. In most cases the data required will come from district patient administration systems which are to be installed in the majority of district general hospitals. It is recognised that some of the smaller or peripheral institutions may lack the benefit of such computerised systems for a time but the management information pilot project in Bromsgrove and Redditch has produced a system which should bridge the gap.

In addition to providing information at district level, it will be essential to safeguard the availability of information at regional and national levels. We must not lose the benefits of HAA and HIPE. The mechanism chosen for the provision of national information is two-pronged, allowing for the central submission of some tabular material as well as data relating to individual episodes of consultant care. By and large, the former will replace the SH3 return and the latter HIPE. It is proposed that data on all hospital consultant episodes will be transmitted centrally to OPCS and analysed there. Some analyses will cover all the records received, others will be on a sample drawn centrally. Responsibility for ensuring completeness and carrying out validation checks will pass to the periphery. Specific guidance on the format for submission of the data required

Michael Alderson and John Ashley

centrally is already available. It is intended that the information collected nationally will be released in a variety of ways to meet the needs of different users.

Conclusion

The review carried out by the Steering Group has established a sound foundation for using information in the 1990s. Although stability in a national system is desirable for economic reasons, the crucial challenge has been to develop systems that will be responsive to changes in medical practice in the future. The Steering Group's approach and methods of work have ensured that a sensible balance has been maintained between continuity and innovation in the production of nationally available information.

REFERENCES

1 Bloom A, Hayes T M, Gamble, D R. Register of newly diagnosed diabetic children. British Medical Journal, 1975, vol 3, no 5983. 580–583.
2 Pedoe H Tunstall, Clayton D, Morris J N, Bridgden W, McDonald L. Coronary heart attacks in East London. The Lancet, 1975 vol 2, no 7940, 833–838.
3 Birmingham Research Unit, RCGP. Influenza. Journal of Royal College of General Practitioners, 1977, vol 27. 544–551.
4 Lee J A H. 'Appendicitis' in young women. The Lancet, 1961, vol 2, no 7206. 815–817.
5 Barker D J P, Donnan S P B. Regional variations in the incidence of upper urinary tract stones in England and Wales. British Medical Journal, 1978, vol 1, no 6105. 67–80.
6 Coggon D, Lambert P, Langman M J S. 20 years of hospital admissions for peptic ulcer in England and Wales. The Lancet, 1981, vol 1, no 8233. 1302–1304.
7 Fraser P, Robinson N, Ashley J S A. The pattern of disease in hospital, 1968–78. Health Trends, 1983, vol 15. 1–6.
8 Barker D J P, Gardner M J. Distribution of Paget's disease in England, Wales, and Scotland and a possible relationship with vitamin D deficiency in childhood. British Journal of Preventive and Social Medicine, 1974, vol 28. 226–232.
9 Williams D R R. Diet and related factors in the aetiology of cerebrovascular disease. In: Smith A, ed. Recent Advances in Community Medicine. Edinburgh, Churchill Livingstone, 1984.
10 Holland W. The study of the geographic differences in the prevalence of chronic bronchitis. Statistician, 1966, vol 16. 5–22.

11 Khot A, Burn R, Evans N, Lenney C, Lenney W. Seasonal variation and time trends in childhood asthma in England and Wales 1975–1981. British Medical Journal, 1984, vol 289. 235–237.

12 Alderson M R. Self-poisoning – what is the future? The Lancet, 1974, vol 1, no 7865. 1040–1043.

13 Alderson M R. Health Information resources – UK health and social factors. In: Holland W W, Detels R, Knox G. eds. vol 31 Textbook of public health. London, Oxford University Press, 1985.

14 Goldacre M J. Hospital inpatient statistics: some aspects of interpretation. Community Medicine, 1981, vol 3, no 1. 60–68.

15 Acheson, E D. Medical record linkage. London, Oxford University Press for Nuffield Provincial Hospitals Trust, 1967.

16 Martini, C J M, Hughes A O, Patton V A. A study of the validity of the Hospital Activity Analysis information. British Journal Preventive and Social Medicine, 1976, vol 30, no 3. 180–186.

17 Department of Health and Social Security. Steering Group on Health Services Information. First Report. A report on the collection and use of information about hospital clinical activity in the National Health Service. (Chairman, Mrs Edith Körner.) London, HMSO, 1982.

18 Department of Health and Social Security. Steering Group on Health Services Information. Converting data into information. London, King's Fund, 1982.

19 Department of Health and Social Security. Steering Group on Health Services Information. Making data credible. London, King's Fund, 1984.

USING INFORMATION

13

Performance indicators

Alan Jennings

The need for NHS performance indicators has always been recognised but never so keenly as it is today. Demands for a more accountable service have made it necessary to answer questions about, for example, the efficient use of resources and their provision in the most appropriate manner; about equality of access to services; and about the degree to which authorities comply with policy decisions. The facts and measurements required to produce indicators are dependent on comprehensive information systems which, in turn, are dependent on the collection of credible data.

Using resources efficiently

From the beginning, the health service has collected plenty of statistical returns and doubtless used some of them. It would be extremely cynical to suggest that all of them have been cast into a vast data graveyard. Nevertheless, the curious and persistent student could be forgiven for wondering why the data were collected when table A 16 of the 1981 report of a 'Study of the Acute Hospital Sector'[1] shows that between regions the range of variation of length of stay in general medicine was from 14.6 to 9.5 days; available beds per thousand varied between 1.0 and 0.4; and discharges and deaths per thousand varied between 22.7 and 11.5. These are regional variations, not district.

What on earth are two-fold variations doing in a national service with regions containing two to five million people; and if the data mean anything, why has nothing been done about what they disclose? It should be pointed out that the boundary between general medicine and geriatrics is so arbitrary and locally idiosyncratic that the data would not necessarily encourage anyone to take action. Nonetheless, whether this charitable view prevails or the harsher judgement that the service is suffering from a paralysis of managerial will, it remains difficult to understand why the data were collected if nothing was to be done with them.

The assembly of statistical returns containing large numbers produced by aggregating lots and lots of little numbers is hardly 'doing something' with the data. All too often the little numbers are due to someone filling in a box on a form with a non-negative integer – a task that may or may not be taken seriously. Results do not obviously flow from this labour, so whether the entry is true, fairly true or false depends on the temperament of the person whose duty it is to fill in the little box. The numbers then ascend the hierarchy of aggregation without further intervention of the human mind, and enjoy their collective apotheosis under the dignified title of 'national statistics'. The absence of intelligence is exemplified by the publication of Table 39 in the Performance Indicators National Summary for 1981[2] which showed the cost per new A & E case varying between £85.80p and 40p. If small departments seeing less than 10,000 new cases per annum are removed, the range was from £54.60p to £3.50p – only a sixteenfold variation!

These differences cannot be explained by current statistics, which do not reflect clinical practice. For example, the range of variation of throughput of patients per bed per annum for general medicine in 1981 was between 49.0 and 17.5. However, in some districts significant numbers of cases are transferred after investigation to outlying supporting hospitals and are counted, under the current rules, as two admissions. Cases transferred to geriatricians are only counted as a discharge to general medicine if transfer into the care of the geriatricians involves a transfer to another hospital. The bed days used before the transfer, however, are always assigned to general medicine. Thus, the mean stay for general medicine is calculated by summing the number of bed days used and dividing them by the number of discharges credited, which is the number of admissions minus the number of transfers to other specialties. This system, devised in 1949, is clearly not relevant to clinical practice in 1985.

Nor are these problems and disparities confined to general medicine. The equivalent figures for general surgery in 1981 were 24.0 to 58.7 patients per bed per annum. But how many of these were pre-convalescent beds in outlying hospitals without operating theatres? How many were in single specialty hospitals without 24-hour cover from on-site medical staff? Unless these questions are answered it is impossible to draw reliable conclusions from the quite startling differences in throughput.

Trauma and orthopaedics showed similar variations, between 11.5 at the lowest to 47.0 at the highest. But is this one specialty or two?; and in how many districts are trauma patients admitted on the site containing the district general hospital and accident department, whereas orthopaedics and some transferred long-stay trauma are on another site? Are the transferred cases double counted? Is there such good liaison and transfer of care between orthopaedics and geriatrics in some districts that bed days are credited to trauma and orthopaedics without any acknowledgement of the case numbers? Many of us would consider a close liaison between orthopaedics and geriatrics (perhaps by joint care, perhaps by transfer of care) to be a forward looking and constructive way to treat the elderly, especially old ladies who fall down and break their femurs. Is it not strange that the current system for recording statistics penalises ortho-paedic surgeons who practise in this fashion?

The deficiencies in current hospital statistics were recognised by the Steering Group[3] and many of the idio-syncrasies have been removed. The identification of con-sultant episodes and their aggregation into hospital stays and district spells will bring reality to reviewing specialty lengths of stay. Each bed day used will be related to the specialty of the consultant actually responsible for care and the total bed days used will be related to the number of patients cared for.

The catch all concept of the 'acute bed' will disappear, as will bed landlords with exclusive rights to certain wards. The new ward classification is according to the types of patient who are intended to use them (for instance, children or the mentally ill) and the intensity of care to be provided in them. Instead of a spurious figure being recorded nightly for the number of beds supposedly available to each spec-ialty, the throughput denominator will be the number of beds district management intend to be used by the specialty.

The introduction of these new data, definitions and class-ifications will bring credibility to traditional indices of hospital performance and permit the in-depth negotiation between management tiers that the accountability reviews demand.

Measuring the balance

Three kinds of balance have to be looked at if reasonable, fair and illuminating performance indicators are to be devised. There has to be a sensible balance between the various resources made available, obtained by examining the ratios within the NHS; a sensible balance between the population served and the resources placed at their dis-posal, obtained by examining the ratios between the service and the world outside; and there is the question of balance over time – the balance between inflow and outflow.

Different types of information are now collected for dif-ferent time bases. Activity information is related to the calendar year and questions about the use made of capital assets, such as the number of patients per bed, have been answered on a different time scale from questions about revenue which depend on the financial year. While the service's third great asset, its manpower, is based on the annual census taken at the midpoint of the financial year. The Steering Group has made recommendations that will greatly facilitate the linking of activity, manpower and financial data, including the production of information on a common time scale.

The linkage of different types of information will also be enhanced by the adoption of common definitions for items of data, no matter whether they are in a manpower, clinical activity or financial information system. Without looking at the balance between capital stock, revenue provision and manpower provision it is impossible to comment intelli-gently on the efficiency of use of any of the clinical or hotel services. The Steering Group proposals put them under one roof, inviting the use of a common language in discus-sions of the service's efficiency.

Resources and a population

The balance between the population served and the resources available can be looked at in two ways. One is to deduce or declare that the proper rate of provision is so much of this, so much of that, per thousand persons served. The other is to look at what is happening over time. Without knowing whether the waiting list is increasing or decreasing it is not easy to deduce what provision is needed, other than by taking a national average and saying 'this works, and if it doesn't, it is all we can afford anyway'.

Chapter 11 of the first report[3] contains recommendations about drawing up the balance sheet for out-patient referrals and for elective admissions. The basic information required is in terms of expressed demand (how many were put on the books), met demand (how many, having been put on were also taken off), attempts to meet demand (how many were offered the service, but could not, did not or would not accept) and unmet demand (how many went on the books, and are still on them). It is essential for monitoring performance in terms of waiting.

To regard the waiting list for elective admission in isolation is naive and it is high time the waiting before being seen as an out-patient was explored. Commenting on the change in the waiting list over a year without knowing what goes on in a year is unhelpful. A clinical service which puts 4,700 people on the waiting list and only manages to take 4,600 off, is probably capable of finding some slack within the organisation with which to achieve a balance. A service which puts 470 on the list and only takes 370 off, is nowhere near being in balance, yet both will show a rise of 100 in the waiting list at the end of the year.

The balance between the population served and the resources made available takes us close to another important purpose of performance indicators; to be assured that there is equality of access to health care or, at any rate, acceptably rapid progress in that direction. There is a large stumbling block here, lurking behind such innocent phrases as 'population served' or 'catchment population' which we all think we understand, but which become more puzzling the more we look at them.

The concept of a catchment population is apparently so simple that the temptation to accept the numbers that pop out of statisticians' calculations and believe they mean something is very great. The raw data for these calculations are the numbers of patients from each district that are treated in each district, specialty by specialty. Often the district of residence and the district of treatment will be the same, but this is not always so, and, especially in conurbations, where more or less arbitrary boundaries separate neighbouring districts rather than green fields, estuaries and moors, the question of measuring cross boundary flows needs to be resolved.

A major difficulty in estimating catchment populations and cross-boundary flows is that methods of calculation which do not depend too much on sample size have an inherent bias which assigns an appearance of extra catchment population to districts which are well resourced and able to sustain higher levels of activity. The method which avoids this bias and provides a fair foundation for just comparisons depends on large, probably 100 per cent samples. The Steering Group's recommendation that OPCS process a 100 per cent sample of consultant episodes will greatly improve the calculation of estimates of catchment population.

The use of performance indicators to examine the degree of compliance with broad policy decisions takes us into questions about the care given to various groups. Present data encourage the assumption that the specialty of a doctor is a sufficient proxy for the classification of patients in his care. For some well defined and discrete groups this might be so – mental handicap is the obvious example – but for others the assumption could well work to the detriment of those for whom policy decisions were made. For example, the care of the elderly is most certainly not confined to the specialty of geriatrics. Attendance at a day care facility and arrangements for an able bodied person to walk to the post office for a pension are meagre substitutes for a successful hip replacement. The recommendations contained in the first and fifth reports[4] recognise these difficulties and avoid vulgar errors like equating the care of the elderly with geriatrics, or the care of children with paediatrics.

Comparison

If performance indicators are to have a constructive impact on the service they must make fair and timely comparisons of things that matter to patients. In order to be unbiased all work must be counted only once. Day cases and ward attenders must be included, as well as innovations in patient management that do not easily fit traditional definitions. The definitions must fit the patterns of patient care, not vice versa. This principle has been observed throughout the Steering Group reports. If equitable comparisons are to be made between districts, like must be compared with like. While many are self-evident geographical entities, others are artefacts made to satisfy local political requirements.

Essentially there are two ways of comparing districts fairly. One is to cluster similar districts together. The difficulty is the likelihood of a fairly large number of clusters, probably more than a dozen though less than a score, and none of equal size – ranging from three or four districts to twenty. This means that comparisons within clusters will often be on a small scale. Without having some way of making comparisons between clusters it is difficult to justify the 'National' in the name of our service.

The second method is to acknowledge the many variations between districts both as to patients and the community services at their disposal. This requires standardised data for which a much richer data base is needed, and the Steering Group's proposals go some way towards providing it. The obvious omission is data about social class which the group decided need not form part of the minimum data set. The collection and classification of these data are skilled tasks requiring training and experience not at present generally available in the NHS. Unless they are done properly any comparisons or deductions made will be liable to error.

Conclusion

It is clear from the disparities revealed by performance indicators based on available data that vast sums of money are being spent in very curious ways. It should be borne in mind, however, that the statistical quirks in the way we currently collect data help vested interests to discount the results. The implementation of the new data sets will remove this traditional excuse for inaction. Provided the managerial and political will exists to act on credible information, the costs of changing the information systems will be minute compared with the benefits. The NHS needs and deserves a better central nervous system. Mrs Körner has provided the afferent input. Will we provide the higher centres?

REFERENCES

1 Department of Health and Social Security. Report of a study of the acute hospital sector. London, DHSS, 1981.
2 Department of Health and Social Security. Performance Indicators National Summary for 1981. London, DHSS, 1983.
3 Department of Health and Social Security. Steering Group on Health Services Information. First Report. A report on the collection and use of information about hospital clinical activity in the National Health Service. (Chairman, Mrs Edith Körner.) London, HMSO, 1982.
4 Department of Health and Social Security. Steering Group on Health Services Information. Fifth Report. A report on the collection and use of information about services for and in the community in the National Health Service. (Chairman, Mrs Edith Körner.) London, HMSO, 1984.

14

Information for members

Christopher Day
and Stuart Haywood

The role of the NHS authority member is set to be a subject of considerable debate in the next few years. Successive reports[1] have discussed the limited impact of many health authorities. The evidence suggests a large gap in most cases between the reality of member contribution and their formal responsibilities. Implementation of the recommendations of the Griffiths report[2] will make this long-standing problem a very live issue. Changes in the content and style of top management and in relationships between top managers can hardly leave members unscathed. Searching questions are inevitable in a political climate characterised by scepticism about the merits and performance of all aspects of public administration.

Authority members

Although its major thrust lay elsewhere, the Griffiths report did have specific things to say about members. Attention was directed to decisions that should be reserved for the health authority itself and to its information requirements. Moreover, the basic philosophy which it prescribed for a NHS management board applies with equal force to authorities: they should be 'passionately concerned with the quality of care and the delivery of services'.[2]

It may be that the required changes will be effected without any particular effort by members. The studies of health authorities by the Health Services Management Centre (HMSC), backed up by work with members, do not give many grounds for optimism on this score. In only two of ten health authorities in the 1982 and 1984 studies did members have a significant or modest influence on local policy making, although some had an impact as individuals. Additionally, business and information frequently owed more to 'incremental drift' than to considered appraisals of role and function.[3]

It is really small wonder. After all, health authorities consist of people with widely differing backgrounds, interests and persuasions who have little to do with each other. Anyone who believed that a common sense of purpose is likely to emerge spontaneously from so disparate a conglomeration would be gravely deluded. Yet emerge it must, if authorities are to command the respect and loyalty of their staff and the confidence of those whom they exist to serve. And if it will not do so spontaneously, it must be made to. Those diverse, caring individuals must be converted into a body of committed people who, besides being the authority, possess authority, the authority that comes from being well informed about what is going on and having a clear view of what they are after.

A forlorn hope? Some health authorities have managed it, with members making contributions valued by all concerned. Others have the potential but somehow have not turned it to maximum effect. Among both groups are authorities which will see the current changes as an opportunity and challenge to do better. For those who take this view, the work of the Steering Group will provide some valuable tools. For the remainder it will be seen as yet another costly, centrally imposed change to be implemented bureaucratically.

Information for members

How might members give greater practical and effective expression to the universal but generalised concern with the quality of service? The post-Griffiths management world will place increasing emphasis on the considered use of statistical information for this purpose by members among others.[1] A district health authority and its officers who are not regularly using statistical data are handicapped by being inadequately informed when fulfilling their responsibilities'.[4]

Tumultuous applause, and rightly so, for how could it be otherwise? Statistical information so obviously complements the information gained in all the other ways. But more than that, it forms the bedrock of factual knowledge upon which sound judgments can be made about the state of the authority's services and the directions in which they should proceed.

Then why is it neglected?

Many authorities may well feel themselves immune from accusations of neglect. After all, do they not receive vast agglomerations of statistics whenever they meet? Indeed they may. And even though the figures may nestle coyly amongst the trifling titbits at the agenda's end, they may provoke the odd question here, some desultory discussion there. But that is a far cry from meaning that they are serving the authority's purpose.

A change of heart is required towards quantitative information. There are good reasons for continued wariness, not the least of which are inaccuracies in the collection of data. Members may also believe that figures can be manipulated in subtle ways to deceive them. They may suspect that the complexities of statistics lie far beyond their comprehension. And they may feel in their bones that crunching numbers is somehow at odds with running a service which is essentially about healing and caring for people in need.

Understandable though they are, barriers such as these to the acceptance of statistical information must be replaced by an understanding of its facility to inform. Yes, statistics can be inaccurate, but the more they are used, the more accurate they will become. Yes, statistics can be made to deceive, but staff can be trusted to present them honestly. Yes, statistics can be incredibly abstruse, but they can also be made entirely straightforward. Above all, statistics are neutral: if they reveal some unwelcome fact, their function has been simply to reveal; the unwelcome fact already existed.

The key to the effective use of statistics lies in doing the obvious – an activity observed rarely in our experience: a systematic consideration of what is required, when and in what form. Such an exercise is by no means all plain sailing. In steering a course through the vast ocean of information it is essential to observe this fundamental rule: the information selected must be directly relevant to the authority's central concerns.

Using information

Just consider a health district. What a vast cauldron of frantic activity it is! Thousands upon thousands of people being born, infected, injured, impregnated, deranged, diseased, demented and in countless other ways registering their need for health care. Members may well feel it relevant to be informed about the characteristics of that seething population, the demands it generates and the ways in which those characteristics and demands are likely to alter with the passage of time.

Next consider the response to those innumerable demands. Knowledgeable indeed are the members who are aware of the full extent of the scores of services provided in the community as well as in the district's hospitals; but how else can they hope to satisfy themselves that every service is doing a good job? Certainly not by peregrinating around the district, however conscientiously.

Once in possession of this factual information, members can turn their attention to their primary concerns; and few would dispute that a basic ingredient of an authority's role is to ensure that its services, if not superb, are at least reasonably acceptable.

The touchstone is quality. And although observation is unsurpassable for assessing, say, the cleanliness of a ward, the comfort of patients or the palatability of food, there is no substitute for statistics when it comes to assessing most of the vitally important aspects of quality.

They can provide essential information to answer such questions as: How effective is a particular service? How responsive is it? How efficiently is it being provided? What is the level of morale amongst those providing it? *Quantitative* information can be produced to illuminate *qualitative* questions.

Consider effectiveness. An effective service is one which succeeds in doing what it exists to do. That presupposes agreement about the aims of each service and the measures of its success. Some measures are well established: levels of infant and maternal mortality, for example, are accepted as being two major measures of obstetric effectiveness; vaccination rates comprise one measure of the effectiveness of the preventive services.

Not all activities may be so amenable to measurement. Members sometimes feel, for example, that they could assess a service's effectiveness if they were told, for each specialty or consultant, the proportion of patients dying in hospital to those discharged; such a measure in fact is fraught with complexities and objections. On the other hand, the proportion of deaths following specific operations could prove a useful indicator if current research, still at an early stage, can be validated.

Members do not have to feel that it is for them to define the aims of the many services or the measures of their effectiveness. It is very much their business, however, to challenge and to agree those definitions and to ensure thereafter that they get to know if a service deteriorates – of which more later.

What of responsiveness? The longer patients wait, the poorer the quality of the service: a fair enough generalisation to justify members in taking a close interest in waiting times. Many authorities do receive details of acute hospital waiting times and waiting lists, and in examining them members are considering two important aspects of their service's ability to respond.

But what of all the other services? How long are crippled elderly people having to wait for their walking sticks, their wheelchairs, the attention of a chiropodist? How long is the wait for an emergency ambulance? Or for the x-ray ordered by a general practitioner?

Members whose views of responsiveness encompass the many services besides those provided in their acute hospitals soon find that their interest may well stimulate a swifter response to the demands upon them.

Efficiency does not of course imply providing a service in which patients are hurried or their treatment is skimped, and sensible members can quickly put paid to any suggestion that by interesting themselves in this crucial aspect of quality they are putting a premium on such conduct.

An efficient service is one which makes a reasonably full and reasonably intensive use of its resources: busy staff, well used accommodation and equipment, all directed towards achieving the service's aims.

Bed occupancy figures have traditionally been authorities' mainstay in assessing efficiency, but what a limited measure they are! True, a low figure may expose the opportunity to reduce waiting times or even to adjust the distribution of beds between specialties (though how often in practice does this happen?). It is the *high* figure that is the great deceiver: it is so often taken to mean that all is well, even though it gives no indication of how intensively the beds are being used. Members who examine *throughput* rates are guarding against making this common error.

But beds are only one of many resources. Consider operating theatres: are they a bottleneck for any of the surgical specialties? Are they in use for a reasonable proportion of the times when they are staffed? Are staff, there or elsewhere, kept on duty for some contingency that only rarely occurs? What of the community services? Could a higher number of community nurses lead to earlier hospital discharge and hence the more intensive use of beds? Is there scope to improve the balance of time spent on home visits and travelling between homes?

The search for the more efficient use of resources pervades the health service. Members who examine the appropriate information are well placed to assess their own staff's success in this endless quest.

Members often express surprise when told that staff morale can be judged from statistical data, and of course, like kindness, compassion and sympathy, it does not lend itself to direct evaluation in this way. But demoralized staff show signs of their unhappiness in two ways: by not coming in to work, and by moving to other jobs. Members who arrange that high absenteeism and turnover rates are brought to their attention are keeping their eyes on vitally important aspects of the quality of their services.

Effectiveness, responsiveness, efficiency, morale: four examples of quality capable of measurement by reference to quantitative information. But something more has to happen to give meaning to the information: it must be put into some sort of context.

Context means comparison: with what has occurred before, with what occurs elsewhere, or with some other yardstick, norm or average. Comparison is an essential ingredient of evaluation, allowing members to judge whether their services are acceptable or in need of attention. And to do this effectively they need to agree the dividing line between what is acceptable and what is not at the outset: they then spare themselves any agonising over whether or not to intervene when they see the figures. This is all about *setting standards*, an activity crucial to every authority concerned about quality. It takes time, care and effort to do properly, but its effect is to give a sense of direction to the district which will inform its activities fundamentally.

Having set those standards, members are in a position to cut through the huge expanse of statistical information about every aspect of every service that would otherwise come their way. They do this simply by saying: tell us only about those services which are below the standards we have set. This combination of standard setting and exception reporting enables authorities to concentrate their attention where it is most needed and ensures that they are not suffocated under the weight of information which – though possibly of interest – does not call for any particular action.

Even relevant information can lose its value, however, if its presentation lacks clarity. Members are busy people who seldom have time to pore over quantities of closely packed figures: yet it is amazing how often they receive statistics in this form. They are entirely reasonable to insist that all the aids to rapid comprehension be used. Statistics can be displayed by means of diagrams, charts or graphs; and computer-based printers can very easily print out the small numbers of copies required in a variety of colours as a further aid to comprehension.

Conclusion

Now what of Edith Körner? The centre stage position that she has occupied has not been one that she has particularly relished. Her driving concern has been to persuade managers to make use of information because it makes sense to do so; because they can see – as she sees so clearly – that information forms the key to a vigorous health service, responsive to the inexorably increasing demands upon it. The prerequisite for such use is a base of sound, integrated and universally collected data, and this has been the central concern of the Steering Group. Complex and involved as this process has been, it is just the starting point, establishing the ground rules before the game begins.

The fruits of Mrs Körner's work now depend on the users, rather than the producers, of information. If authority members rise to this challenge, they will be doing the NHS an inestimable service. They will also be helping to still doubts – at present no more than a whisper – as to whether their contribution is truly effective.

REFERENCES

1 Royal Commission on the NHS. The working of the NHS. (Chairman, Sir Alec Merrison.) London, HMSO, 1978. Research paper no 1.
2 Department of Health and Social Security. NHS management inquiry. (Leader, Mr Roy Griffiths.) London, DHSS, 1983.
3 Haywood S C, Ranade W. District Health Authorities in action: two years on. Birmingham Health Services Management Centre, 1985.
4 Department of Health and Social Security. Steering Group on Health Services Information. Converting data into information. London, King's Fund, 1982.

15

Using information

John Yates

Why don't people use information? The classic answer is that the information is not good enough. Students of information systems will list characteristics expected of 'good' information. It has to be accurate, complete, relevant, timely, well presented and so on. Both information theorists[1] and practical researchers[2,3] have reviewed the inadequacies of information systems, and their findings are accepted in whole or in part by clinicians and managers in the NHS. The latter can substantiate the work of the theorist and researcher by quoting many anecdotal examples of information failure. It is conventional wisdom and common belief that NHS information systems are totally inadequate.

Both the pessimist and the optimist react to such criticisms by deciding that information systems need to be redesigned in order to secure the necessary improvements. It is only when we get down to such an exercise that we begin to realise that some characteristics agreed to be important appear to be self-contradictory. To attain complete accuracy, can mean losing timeliness. Most of the desirable characteristics are not achievable without trading one off against the other, and those who set out to redesign information systems very soon realise that whatever they choose is going to be far from perfect. Quite often the redesigned system is closer to the existing system than we are prepared to admit.

Slowly the truth begins to dawn. The classic answer to the question of why people fail to use information is actually incorrect. Managers and clinicians excuse themselves for failing to use information, repeating like parrots the problems of inaccuracy, incompleteness, untimeliness and irrelevance. The real answer to why people fail to use information is that it is *they* who aren't good enough. Indeed, it is dangerous to say 'they'. We are the managers and clinicians who designed and use our current information systems. It is you and I who fail to feed in accurate data, fail to check the information that we have got, and fail to present it in a timely and readable manner. The fact is that all too often it is we who are either unable or unwilling to use the data. The textbooks, the slides, the conference speeches and the anecdotes about accuracy, completeness, timeliness and relevance are all symptoms. The real illness is our inability and unwillingness. Let us look at a few examples that illustrate this problem. Do you remember the following? 'In spite of the comprehensive returns of staff and facilities submitted annually to both the department and the board, deficiencies shown at the hospital have apparently led to no positive action.' Most of us would be hard pressed to know which hospital enquiry that was. The only clue is the use of 'board' instead of 'authority', which tells us that it was before 1974. It was in fact the Whittingham enquiry of 1972, but it could have been any mental hospital enquiry in the last 20 years. Year after year, health authorities at district, area and regional level and the Department of Health have consistently ignored data collected to help monitor these very situations. At least the Whittingham enquiry report commented on the failure to use information; most enquiry reports do not even mention it. Not only do health authorities not bother with comparative information, but neither do most of the teams of enquiry. Having failed to use the data for so many years we now attempt to cover up our inefficiency by allowing a Rayner review[4] to recommend that the collection should cease.

In 1979 Professor Duthie's working party on orthopaedic services[5] asked for data about orthopaedic and trauma services on a district by district basis across the country. Members of the working party discovered that there was some information which could have been made available, but never had, and other necessary information which was simply unavailable. There were no records that the DHSS could lay hands on that could explain how many consultants worked in each district and what their contractual sessions were. There were no comparative data in the NHS about theatres, nor about out-patient waiting time! The working party was duly indignant and recommended that these problems be rectified, but the NHS still has no data on some of these subjects and we have to rely on ad hoc studies by the British Medical Association[6] and the Medical Architecture Research Unit[7] to glimpse variations in out-patient waiting times and theatre utilisation across the country. NHS management has been unable to get hold of data that outside organisations simply elicit by questionnaire.

131

In 1967 the first cogwheel report[8] recommended that clinicians be helped to undertake a continuous review of hospital activity at divisional level and to take an active part in the coordination and planning of services, including the use of beds and out-patient services. Four years later, Forsyth and Sheikh[9] discovered that very little progress had been made and that expectations for the better provision and use of information were limited. Now the situation is no better, and it is the exception rather than the rule to find a medical staff structure which actively examines information. This is principally the fault of NHS administration.

For nearly twenty years now hospital activity analysis (HAA) has been widely criticised and even ridiculed by the medical profession and hospital administrators. Many regard it as very inaccurate and most think it totally useless. The studies that have examined HAA data, showing enormous variations in length of stay and death rate, are frequently disregarded because of doubts about their accuracy. Having used HAA data for twenty years I have to offer a different opinion. HAA data, despite their inaccuracies, identify very significant variations in practice. They are embarrassing to the medical profession, and management is too frightened to explore some of the issues raised. Consultant by consultant and district by district in this country you find up to ten fold variations in death rates for individual diagnoses and operations. With a death rate for gall bladder operations varying between 0.3 per cent and 4 per cent presumably you do not mind to which hospital you are admitted because HAA is inaccurate? Maybe clinicians and managers will accept this, but consumer organisations will not. For too many people, HAA is inaccurate and that is the way they like it.

Will the Körner review improve things?

Ironically, the Steering Group started by doing two things to hinder the process of improvement. It very clearly identified the deficiencies of the existing systems and thus reinforced prejudices about the uselessness of information. It also gave clinicians and managers a wonderful excuse for inaction because any decision could be put off while information was under review, and there might be a change of data system.

It was not long, however, before the tide began to turn with a vengeance. Firstly, the Steering Group helped the NHS to understand that no information system is perfect and that trade offs have to be made between some of the desirable characteristics. Secondly, some of the perceived difficulties, which I suggest are symptoms, were quickly identified. The group has highlighted and promoted training and education as a means of ensuring that staff not only know how to collect data but know why they are doing it. Thirdly, the group began to bring the NHS – screaming – into the twentieth century by revealing some of the advantages of modern information technology. Of course, it is unwise to over-emphasise the value of information technology, lest it be thought the cure for all ills, but the King's Fund series of publications has shown how the technology can be applied to district problems.[10,11,12] Fourthly, and most importantly, the group's work has encouraged an unprecedented discussion on information systems and their use, occasionally provoking and upsetting people. The Steering Group has provided a much improved data base. Step one is virtually complete; our task is to take step two.

How can we improve things?

The review of data content is just a starting point. Much more remains to be done. I would like to recommend four difficult tasks. Put crudely, they are: stop whining, resist distractions, try measuring a problem and be shocked by inequity.

The Steering Group's recommendations have been met quite rightly by constructive and destructive criticism. Now we are at the stage of implementing the recommendations which have stood the test of criticism. If you have failed to modify a Steering Group report to suit your own prejudices it is time to shut up. Constant whining slows progress. It is difficult enough to create enthusiasm for implementing new systems without having to contend with sceptical and be-grudging support as well. From now on the going will get tough; if you can't stand the heat, get out of the kitchen.

We have a complex health service which is one of Europe's largest employers and has an enormous expenditure. The problems that arise with budgets, re-organisations, cleaning contracts, consultation procedures and thousands of other issues must not be allowed to distract attention from vital matters like testing the efficacy and effectiveness of the preventative and curative services the NHS is here to provide. We are in danger of developing a superb micro-computer budgeting system enabling us to accurately cost gastric freezing (of the stomach), but failing to tell the accountant that the operation is completely useless. Concentrate information systems on issues directly relevant to patients and the health of communities.

O'Neill[13] wrote: 'Knowing the size of the problem is the first step to doing something about it.' Neither our existing data, nor the new data sets were designed for fun or to reduce unemployment. Information is there to be used in order to solve problems and even identify problems. Information systems are never perfect, but they soon become very imperfect when not used. The Steering Group's work will have been to no avail if we cannot show how parts of the information set can be used to identify problems. Go and measure a problem.

Finally, a national information system enables us to compare performance. We have not so much a National Health Service as a collection of local health services. Their stand-ards and achievements vary enormously and our informa-tion systems already demonstrate that dramatically. The new data sets will confirm and clarify that inequity, but do not assume that variation is due to imperfect data defini-tions. Do not relax in the comforting thought that we cannot all be the same. Be shocked by the fact that similar hospitals can have a threefold variation in staffing levels and that there are wards today where one nurse looks after thirty patients. Be shocked that in one district you can get an orthopaedic out-patients appointment next week and in another, next year. Be shocked into checking the data and then achieving a change for the better.

But what about the costs?

Using information is costly. Are you and I prepared to pay the price?

1. To establish and run a good information system is expensive. If additional money is not forthcoming are you prepared to take it from elsewhere in your budget?
2. It will cost time and effort to obtain and use the information. Will you ensure that time is found to gather data accurately, to analyse them and to present them to the appropriate users?
3. It will mean self-sacrifice. Are you prepared to change your working methods if the analysis of the information points to the need for change?
4. It will cost friendship in forcing through unwelcome change. Are you ready for that?

Edith Körner has paid some of these costs. She recognised from the outset that 'spring cleaning' the NHS information system would be a mammoth task, and probably completely thankless. It must have been hard work for someone whose career as a member and chairman of various health authorities has been notable for care of people, not statistics. In common with Florence Nightingale, Edith Körner recognised that improved information strengthens the case for improved patient care, although it does not, of course, guarantee it. That is our task.

REFERENCES

1 Ackoff R L and Emery F E. On purposeful systems. London, Tavistock Publications, 1972.
2 McNeilly R H and Moore F. The accuracy of some Hospital Activity Analysis data. Hospital and Health Services Review, 1975, vol 7, no 3. 93–95.
3 Martini C J M, Hughes A O and Patton V A. A study of the validity of Hospital Activity Analysis information. British Journal Preventive and Social Medicine, 1976, vol 30, no 3. 180–186.

John Yates

4 Department of Health and Social Security. Review of mental health statistics, report of review team. London, DHSS, 1980.
5 Department of Health and Social Security. Orthopaedic services: waiting time for out-patient appointments and in-patient treatment. Report of a working party. (Chairman, Prof. R B Duthie.) London, HMSO, 1981.
6 Hyde A Minister 'surprised' by BMA's disclosure on waiting lists. Health and Social Services Journal, 1984, vol 94. 1101.
7 The Polytechnic of North London, Medical Architecture Research Unit. An evaluation of the provision and utilisation of operating theatre suites, summary report. June 1981.
8 Ministry of Health. First report of the joint working party on the organisation of medical work in hospitals. (Chairman, Sir George Godber.) London, HMSO, 1967.
9 Forsyth G and Sheikh J M. The mechanics of medical management. In: McLachlan G ed. In low gear? an examination of 'Cogwheels's. London, Oxford University Press, 1971. 1–53.
10 Department of Health and Social Security. Steering Group on Health Services Information. Converting data into information. London, King's Fund, 1982.
11 Department of Health and Social Security. Steering Group on Health Services Information. Introducing IT in the district office. London, King's Fund, 1983.
12 Department of Health and Social Security. Steering Group on Health Services Information. Developing a district IT policy. London, King's Fund, 1983.
13 O'Neill, P. Health Crisis 2000. London, Heinemann Medical, 1983.

BIBLIOGRAPHY

The NHS/DHSS Health Services Information Steering Group

A. REPORTS TO THE SECRETARY OF STATE

These contain recommendations about the data content of the NHS information systems; available from Her Majesty's Stationery Office, 49 High Holborn, London WC1V 6HB.

The First Report; the collection and use of information about hospital clinical activity.
Published in 1982
The Second Report; the collection and use of information about patient transport services.
Published in 1984
The Third Report; the collection and use of information about health services manpower.
Published in 1984
The Fourth Report; the collection and use of information about activity in hospitals and the community.
Published in 1984
The Fifth Report; the collection and use of information about services for and in the community.
Published in 1984
The Sixth Report; the collection and use of information about health services finance.
Published in 1984
The Supplement to the First and Fourth Reports; the collection and use of information about maternity services.
Published in 1985

B. WORKING GROUP REPORTS

These are available from the Health Services Information Branch, DHSS, Euston Tower, 286 Euston Road, London NW1

A Report from the Confidentiality Working Group; the protection and maintenance of confidentiality of patient and employee data.
Published in 1984
The Interim Report of the Dental Working Group; the collection and use of information about dental services.
Published in 1985

Bibliography

C. BOOKS AND OCCASIONAL PAPERS

These contain proposals for improving the environment in which data are collected and information is used. They are available from the King's Fund Centre, 126 Albert Street, London NW1 7NF.

Book
From figures to facts. Christopher Day.
Published in 1985

Papers
Converting data into information; the management arrangements for collecting valid clinical data and setting up a district information service.
Published in 1982
Introducing IT in the district office; a study carried out in one health district.
Published in 1983
Developing a district IT policy; the development of a district policy for the introduction of IT with particular emphasis on the implementation of computerised departmental systems.
Published in 1983
Piloting Körner; the views of administrators who piloted the Körner data sets.
Published in 1984
Making data credible; the setting, achieving and monitoring of data standards with particular emphasis on standards for clinical activity data.
Published in 1984
Enabling clinical work; the organisational arrangements required to enable hospital clinical work, based on studies done in five districts.
Published in 1985
Providing a district library service; the contribution library services can make to the provision and use of information in the NHS.
Published in 1985